Residential Inspector's Guide
Building Provisions, Chapters 1-10

ISBN # 1-58001-158-6

COPYRIGHT © 2005
by
INTERNATIONAL CODE COUNCIL, INC.

ALL RIGHTS RESERVED. This publication is a copyrighted work owned by the International Code Council, Inc. Without advance written permission from the copyright owner, no part of this book may be reproduced, distributed, or transmitted in any form or by any means, including, without limitation, electronic, optical or mechanical means (by way of example and not limitation, photocopying, or recording by or in an information storage retrieval system). For information on permission to copy material exceeding fair use, please contact: Publications, 4051 West Flossmoor Road, Country Club Hills, IL 60478-5795 (Phone 888-422-7233).

Information contained in this work has been obtained by the author and the International Code Council (ICC) from sources believed to be reliable. Neither ICC nor its authors shall be responsible for any errors, omissions, or damages arising out of this information. This work is published with the understanding that ICC and its authors are supplying information but are not attempting to render engineering or other professional services. If such services are required, the assistance of an appropriate professional should be sought.

Publication Date: June 2005
First printing: June 2005
Second printing: November 2005

PRINTED IN THE U.S.A.

Preface
Residential Inspector's Guide
Building Provisions, Chapters 1-10

The duties of an inspector are extensive and varied; however, the primary function continues to be the verification that construction work complies with the codes and policies adopted by the jurisdiction. As many other responsibilities are placed upon the inspector, it is necessary that he or she develop an efficient and effective approach to the inspection process. This inspector's guide is designed to assist the inspector in verifying code compliance by identifying many of the more common code requirements. The guide provides the code in a checklist format, identifying not only the code provisions, but also the appropriate references in the *International Residential Code*® (IRC®). The use of a checklist can be a valuable tool for a building safety department for:

1. Providing consistency within the department when all of the inspectors are using the same criteria;
2. Serving as a training method for new employees or to assist in the updating of existing staff members on new code provisions;
3. Providing builders, particularly homeowner builders, with an easy-to-use document to assist them in complying with the code; and
4. Assisting the inspectors in staying focused and not overlooking items during their inspections.

This *Residential Inspector's Guide: Based on the 2003 International Residential Code,* only includes requirements from Chapters 1 through 10 of the IRC, which are generally referred to as the "building provisions." Its consistent use can be an important asset during inspection activities.

Table of Contents

Inspection Preparation	1
Footings and Foundations	2
Foundation Walls	9
Floors	19
Location on Lot	29
Light, Ventilation and Heating	29
Room Heights and Areas	31
Glazing	32
Garages and Carports	34
Escape and Rescue Openings	34
Means of Egress	35
Stairways	36
Guards	39
Smoke Alarms	39
Dwelling Unit Separations	40
Wood Wall Framing	45
Fireblocking	47
Wall Bracing	48
Steel Wall Framing	52
Masonry Construction	57
ICF Walls	72

Exterior Windows and Glass Doors	81
Interior Wall Coverings	83
Exterior Covering	86
Exterior Veneer	90
Wood Roof Framing	96
Steel Roof Framing	102
Roof Coverings	110
Reroofing	120
Masonry Chimneys	122
Masonry Fireplaces	126

INSPECTION PREPARATION

INSPECTION PREPARATION

- All materials, equipment and devices shall be approved by the building official.

R104.9

- Modifications to code provisions shall be approved by the building official.

R104.10

- Any variance in requirements to projects in areas prone to flooding shall only be granted by the Board of Appeals.

R104.10.1

- Alternative materials, design or methods of construction and equipment shall be approved by the building official.

R104.11

- Permit(s) shall be issued prior to project beginning and fees shall be paid.

R105.1 & R108

- Permits shall be reviewed to determine if they are still valid due to elapsed time, delay in starting or permit expiration.

R105.3.2, R105.3.4, R105.5 & R105.6

- Phased construction shall be approved by the building official.

R106.3.3

- Information for construction in areas prone to flooding shall be submitted and approved.

R106.1.3

- Building official shall approve temporary utility connection.

R111.2

- Buildings and structures shall comply with all provisions of the code.

R301.1

- Buildings exceeding the limits of Section 301 shall be designed in accordance with accepted engineering practices.

R103.1

FOOTINGS AND FOUNDATIONS

- A building permit or copy shall be on the job site.

    R105.7

- Construction documents shall be on the job site.

    R106.3.1

- Site plan shall show size and location of the new and existing construction.

    R106.2

- Excavation shall be completed, forms shall be in place and reinforcing steel, when required, shall be in place.

    R109.1.1

- Fill soils shall be designed, installed and tested in accordance with accepted engineering practices.

    R401.2

- Gravel fill used as footings for wood and precast concrete foundations shall comply with Section R403.

- Concrete shall have compressive strength.

    R402.2

- Approved precast concrete foundations shall be designed and installed per this code and manufacturers' installation instructions.

- Continuous footings shall be provided for braced wall panels in Seismic Design Category (SDC) D_1 and D_2 at exterior walls and interior walls exceeding 50 feet (15 240 mm) in plan dimension.

    R403.1.2

- Reinforcement steel for footing in SDC D_1 or D_2 shall comply with Section R403.1.3.

- There shall be a minimum of 3 inches (76 mm) that is clear from the bottom of the footing.

- Minimum one vertical No. 4 rebar shall be used for positive connection between footing and foundation; vertical No. 4 rebar shall not be more than 4 feet (1219 mm) on center; extend 3 inches (76 mm) clear of bottom of footing; have a standard hook and extend a minimum of 14 inches (357 mm) into the stem wall.

    R403.1.3

FOOTINGS

FOOTINGS

I. Concrete and Masonry Footings

- Concrete and masonry footings shall comply with Figure R403.1(1) and Table 403.1.

- Spread footings shall be at least 6 inches (152 mm) in thickness.

R403.1.1

- Footing projections shall be at least 2 inches (51 mm) and shall not exceed thickness of footing.

R403.1.1

- Footings shall extend below the frost line, and exterior footings shall be at least 12 inches (305 mm) below undisturbed ground. See exceptions.

R403.1.4

- The top surface of footings shall be level.

R403.1.5

- Maximum slope for the bottom of footing shall not exceed 10 percent; 1:10 without steps.

R403.1.5

- Stepped footings shall be required when the slope exceeds 10 percent (1:10).

R403.1.5

- In SDC D_1 and D_2, minimum one vertical No. 4 rebar not more than 4 feet (1219 mm) on the center shall be used; the vertical rebar shall extend to 3 inches (76 mm) clear of bottom and shall have a standard hook.

R403.1.3

- Masonry stem walls shall not be permitted without solid grout and vertical reinforcement in SDC D_1 and D_2. See exceptions.

R403.1.3

- Two bars of steel are required for foundation with stem walls in SDC D_1 and D_2: one No. 4 at the top and one No. 4 at the bottom.

R403.1.3.1

- One No. 4 bar is required at the top and bottom of footing for slab-on-ground turned down footing in SDC D_1 and D_2. See exceptions.

R403.1.3.2

3

- Interior footings supporting bearing or shear walls and cast monolithically with the slab shall have a minimum depth of 18 inches (457 mm) in SDC D_1 and D_2.

    R403.1.4

II. Wood Foundations and Footings

- Foundations and footings shall comply with Figures R403.1(2) and R403.1(3).

    R402.1.1

- Type 304 or 316 stainless steel fasteners shall be used to attach plywood to exterior side of wall studs or knee wall construction.

    R402.1.1

- Type 304 or 316 stainless steel, silicon bronze, copper, hot dipped or hot tumbled steel nails shall be used for above grade attachment.

    R402.1.1

- Electrogalvanized steel nails and galvanized (zinc coated) steel staples shall not be permitted.

    R402.1.1

- All lumber and plywood shall be labeled.

    R402.1.2

- All lumber and plywood cut or drilled after treatment shall be field treated with Copper Naphthenate, which shall contain a minimum 2-percent copper metal.

    R402.1.2

- Footings shall comply with Figures R403.1(2) and (3).

    R403.2

- Gravel shall be washed and well graded.

    R403.2

- Maximum stone shall not exceed ¾ inch (19.1 mm).

    R403.2

- Gravel shall be free of organic, clayey or silty soils.

    R403.2

- Sand shall be coarse, free from organic, clayey or silty soils and not smaller than $1/16$ inch (1.6 mm) grains.

    R403.2

- Crushed stone shall be a maximum size of ½ inch (12.7 mm).

    R403.2

WOOD FOUNDATIONS

FOUNDATION ANCHORAGE

III. Foundation Anchorage

- Anchor bolts shall be spaced a maximum of 6 feet (1829 mm) on center.

R403.1.6

- There shall be two anchor bolts: Two bolts per plate section, one not more than 12 inches (305 mm) or less than seven bolt diameters from each end.

R403.1.6

- Anchor bolts shall be a minimum of $\frac{1}{2}$ inch (12.7 mm) in diameter and extend a minimum of 7 inches (178 mm) into concrete or masonry.

R403.1.6

- Nut and washer required for each bolt.

R403.1.6

- Sills and sole plates shall be protected against decay and termites when required by Section R322 or R323. See exceptions.

- Anchor bolts shall be used on all exterior walls and interior braced wall lines (SDC D_1 and D_2 only).

R403.1.6

- Plate washers for anchor bolts shall be 3 inches by 3 inches by $\frac{1}{4}$ inch (76 mm by 76 mm by 6.4 mm) thick in SDC D_1 and D_2, also C for townhouses.

R602.11.1

- Anchor bolts shall be spaced not more than 4 feet (1219 mm) on center for two-story buildings in SDC D_1 and D_2, also C for townhouses.

R403.1.6.1

IV. Footings on or Adjacent to Slopes

NOTE: These provisions shall comply with Section 403.1.7 when slope is steeper than 1:3 (33.3 percent slope):

A. Ascending slope

- The setback to face of structure shall be one-half the height of slope but not more than 15 feet (4572 mm) maximum.

R403.1.7.1

- Slopes that exceed 100-percent slope (1:1) shall have toe of slope designated at the intersection of a horizontal plane drawn from top of foundation and plane drawn tangent to slope at 45-degree angle.

- Height of slope shall be measured from top of foundation wall; if foundation is constructed at the toe, it shall be measured to the top of slope.

    R403.1.7.1

B. Descending slope

- The setback from face of footing to slope shall be one-third the height of the slope but not more than 40 feet (12 192 mm) maximum.

    R403.1.7.2

- Slopes that exceed 100 percent slope (1:1) shall have required setback measured from imaginary plane 45 degrees from horizontal projected up from toe of slope.

    R403.1.7.2

C. Foundation elevation

- Foundation shall be 12 inches (305 mm) plus 2 percent above elevation of street gutter on graded sites.

    R403.1.7.4

- Alternative elevations shall be approved by the building official provided drainage complies.

    R403.1.7.3

D. Alternative setbacks and clearances

- Building official shall approve alternative setbacks and clearances.

    R403.1.7.4

- Investigation and recommendation of qualified engineer shall include materials, height of slope, slope grade, loads and erosion characteristics—building official approval is required.

    R403.1.7.4

V. Drainage

- Surface drainage shall be diverted to storm sewer or other approved collection.

    R401.3

- Lots shall be graded to drain water away from foundation; 6 inches (152 mm) within first 10 feet (3048 mm).

    R401.3

- Drains or swales shall be provided whenever barriers prevent 6 inches (152 mm) of fall within first 10 feet (3048 mm).

    R 401.3

SOIL TESTS

VI. Soil Tests

- Table R401.4.1 shall be used for presumptive load-bearing values.

R401.4

- Building official shall determine if soil test is required. A test is required where compressive, shifting or expansive soils are likely.

R401.5

- Soils shall be removed if they are compressible or shifting, and shall not be used as fill.

R401.5

- Foundations on expansive soils shall comply with Section 1805.8 of the *International Building Code*® (IBC®).

R403.1.8

- Building official required to approve slab-on-ground or other foundation systems that have performed adequately in similar conditions.

R403.1.8

- Soils shall be considered to be expansive when all four items or only Item 4 of Section R403.1.8.1 are met.

R403.1.8

VII. Frost-Protected Shallow Foundations

- Footings shall comply with Section R403.3(1) and Table 403.3.

R403.3

- Gravel shall be washed and well graded.

R403.3

- Maximum size of any stone shall not exceed ¾ inch (19.1 mm).

R403.3

- Gravel shall be free of organic, clayey or silty soils.

R403.3

- Sand shall be coarse, free from organic, clayey or silty soils and not smaller than $^{1}/_{16}$ inch (1.6 mm) grains.

R403.3

- Crushed stone shall be a maximum size of ½ inch (12.7 mm).

R403.3

- Permitted for buildings where monthly mean temperature of building is maintained at 64°F (18°C) maximum.

  R403.3

- Footings are not required to extend below frost line when protected in accordance with Figure R403.3(1) and Table R403.3.

  R403.3

- Attachment to unheated slab-on-ground permitted when complying with Section R403.3.1.1:
  1. Insulation complies with Figure R403.3(3) and Table R403.3;
  2. Vertical insulation between frost protected foundation and adjoining slab foundation;
  3. Horizontal insulation shall be continuous.

  R403.3

- Materials used below grade shall be labeled as complying with ASTM C 578.

  R403.3

- Horizontal insulation placed less than 12 inches (305 mm) below surface shall be protected.

  R403.3.2

- Horizontal insulation extending outward more than 24 inches shall be protected.

  R403.3.2

- Protection for insulation shall be:
  1. Concrete slab.
  2. Asphalt paving.
  3. Cementitious board.
  4. Plywood, rated for below-ground use.
  5. Other approved materials placed below ground, directly above top of insulation.

  R403.3.2

- Final grade shall be 6 inches (152 mm) within the first 10 feet (3048 mm) or alternative as approved by the building official.

  R403.3.2

- Gravel or crushed stone used beneath horizontal insulation shall drain to daylight or approved sewer system.

  R403.3.2

- Use of foam plastic in areas of "very heavy" termite infestation shall be in accordance with Section R324.4.

  R403.3.3

FROST-PROTECTED SHALLOW FOUNDATIONS

GENERAL FOUNDATION REQUIREMENTS

FOUNDATION WALLS

- Foundation walls shall comply with Section R404 or ACI 318, NCMA TR68-A or ACI 530/ASCE 5/TMS 402 or other approved standards.
- Unless required by state law, the seal of the architect or engineer is not required for construction documents when the above approved standards are used.

R404.1

- Wood foundations shall be in accordance with AF&PA Report No. 7 with two permitted exceptions.

R404.1

- Wood foundations in SDC D_1 and D_2 shall be designed in accordance with accepted engineering practice.
- Concrete masonry and clay masonry foundations shall comply with:
  1. Table R404.1.1(1) – Plain concrete and plain masonry.
  2. Table R404.1.1(2) – 8-inch (203 mm) reinforced concrete and masonry.
  3. Table R404.1.1(3) – 12-inch (305 mm) reinforced concrete and masonry.
  4. Table R404.1.1(4) – 10-inch (254 mm) reinforced concrete and masonry.

Verify the following:

1. Maximum wall height.
2. Maximum unbalanced backfill height.
3. Type of soil.
4. Soil classes.
5. Minimum reinforcement.
6. Footnotes.

- Design in accordance with accepted engineering practices shall be provided whenever walls are subject to hydrostatic pressure from groundwater or if walls support more than 48 inches (1219 mm) of unbalanced backfill without having permanent lateral support at the top and bottom.

R404.1.3

I. Foundation Walls in SDC D$_1$ and D$_2$

- Walls shall have one No. 4 rebar in upper 12 inches (305 mm) of wall.

    R404.1.4

- Walls shall have 8 feet (2438 mm) maximum wall height.

    R404.1.4

- Walls shall have 4 feet (1219 mm) maximum unbalanced backfill.

    R404.1.4

- Foundation walls shall have 7½-inches (191 mm) minimum thickness, except 6 inches (152 mm) permitted for 4 feet 6 inches (1372 mm) maximum high wall.

    R404.1.4

- Walls shall have a minimum 8-inch (203 mm) No. 3 bar, 4 feet (1220 mm) maximum on center in grouted walls and tied to horizontal rebar in footings.

    R404.1.4

- Foundation walls shall comply with Tables R404.1.1(2), (3) and (4) when supporting more than 4 feet (1219 mm) of unbalanced fill or exceeding 8 feet (2438 mm) in height.

    R404.1.4

- Minimum reinforcement shall be two No. 4 horizontal bars located in the upper 12 inches (305 mm) of the wall.

    R404.1.4

- Foundation walls shall not be less than thickness of wall supported. See exception.

    R404.1.4

- Wall thickness shall be 8 inches (203 mm) minimum for plain masonry wall.

    R404.1.4

- Vertical steel shall be minimum one No. 3 bar, feet (1220 mm) maximum on center in grouted walls and tied to horizontal rebar in footings.

    R404.1.4

- Foundation walls shall comply with Tables R404.1.1(2), (3) and (4) when supporting more than 4 feet (1219 mm) of unbalanced fill or exceeding 8 feet (2438 mm) in height.

    R404.1.4

CONCRETE AND MASONRY FOUNDATION WALLS 11

- Minimum reinforcement shall be two No. 4 horizontal bars located in the upper 12 inches (305 mm) of the wall.

R404.1.4

II. Concrete and Masonry Foundation Walls

- Foundation walls shall not be less than thickness of wall supported. See exception.

R404.1.5

- Maximum height of wall shall not exceed 20 feet (6096 mm)

R404.1.5

A. Pier and curtain wall foundations permitted for light-frame construction not more than two stories in height.

- Load-bearing walls shall be continuous footings integral with exterior footings.

R404.1.5.1

- Walls shall be 4 inches (102 mm) nominal [$3^3/_8$ inch (92 mm) actual], bonded with piers per Section R606.8 minimum actual thickness.

R404.1.5.1

- Piers shall be bonded into load-bearing masonry walls per Sections R608.1.1 and R608.1.2.

R404.1.5.1

- There shall be 4-feet (1219 mm) maximum height for 4-inch (102 mm) load-bearing masonry foundation supporting wood framed walls and floors.

R404.1.5.1

- Anchorage shall be per Section R403.1.6 and Figure 404.1.5(1) or have engineered design approved by the building official.

R404.1.5.1

- There shall be 24-inches (610 mm) maximum unbalanced fill for hollow masonry wall.

R404.1.5.1

- In SDC D_1 and D_2, horizontal joint minimum reinforcement shall be two No. 9 gage wires spaced no less than 6 inches (152 mm) or one ¼-inch (6.4 mm) wire at 10 inches (254 mm) on center vertically. (Vertical shall be one No. 4 bar.)

R404.1.5.1

- Height above finished grade shall be 4 inches (102 mm) maximum for masonry veneer and 6 inches (152 mm) minimum for all others.

  R404.1.6

- Backfill shall not be placed against the wall until the wall has sufficient strength, it has been anchored to floor above or it has been braced to prevent damage from backfill. See exceptions.

  R404.1.6

- Rubble stone masonry shall have 16 inches (406 mm) minimum thickness, shall not support unbalanced backfill exceeding 8 feet (2438 mm) in height, shall not support soil pressure greater than 30 pounds per square foot (psf) (1436 Pa) and shall not be constructed in SDC D_1 and D_2.

  R404.1.6

B. Foundation waterproofing and dampproofing

- Waterproofing is required in areas of high-water table or where other severe-water conditions exist.

  R406

- Waterproofing is used to protect below-grade habitable or useable spaces.

  R406

- Approved waterproofing shall be applied.

  R406

- Dampproofing is required to protect below-grade habitable or useable space not required to be waterproofed.

  R406

- Approved dampproofing shall be applied.

  R406

C. Foundation drainage

- Drains shall be required around foundations that retain earth and enclose habitable and useable space below grade.

  R405.1

- Drains to be installed at or below area are to be protected.

  R405.1

- Drains shall discharge by gravity or mechanical means to approved drain.

  R405.1

DAMPPROOFING AND WATERPROOFING

WOOD FOUNDATION WALLS

- Gravel/crushed stone drains shall extend 1 foot (305 mm) beyond footing and 6 inches (153 mm) above footing.

R405.1

- Gravel/crushed stone drains shall be covered with approved filter fabric.

R405.1

- The top of open joints of drain tiles shall be protected.

R405.1

- Drainage tiles/perforated pipe shall be placed on a minimum of 2 inches (51 mm) and covered with no less than 6 inches (153 mm) of washed gravel or crushed rock. See exceptions.

R405.1

II. Wood Foundation Walls

- Walls shall be identified by grade mark or have certificate of inspections.

R404.2.2

- Walls shall have 2-inch by 6-inch (51 mm by 152 mm) studs, F_b shall not be less than 1250, spaced 16 inches (406 mm) on center.

R404.2.2

- Studs spaced 12 inches (305 mm) on center shall have F_b not less than 875 required.

R404.2.2

A. Backfill

- Maximum height of backfill for wood foundations not designed/built to AF&PA No. 7 shall not exceed 4 feet (1219 mm).

R404.2.3

- Maximum height of backfill above interior grade of crawl space or floor of basement shall be 12 inches (305 mm) or shall comply with Table R404.2.3. Use Table R404.2.3 for plywood grade and thickness when fill exceeds 12 inches (305 mm).

R404.2.3

- Wood foundation walls shall not be backfilled until basement floor and first floor have been constructed or walls have been braced.

R404.2.4

13

- Crawl space walls shall have backfill or bracing installed on interior of walls prior to backfilling exterior.

    R404.2.4

- Wood foundations shall be drained and dampproofed per Sections R405 and R406.

    R404.2.4

- Wood panel wall sheathing shall be attached per Section R402.1.1 and Table R602.3(1).

    R404.2.4, .5, .6

- Sill plates shall be minimum 2-inch by 4-inch (51 mm by 102 mm) nominal lumber.

    R404.3

B. Dampproofing wood foundations

- Dampproofing is required for habitable or useable space located below grade.

    R406

- Panel joints shall be sealed.

    R406

- Moisture barrier shall be applied.

    R406

- Porous fill shall be in place.

    R406

- Backfill shall be same type of soil removed during excavation.

    R406

C. Wood foundation drainage

- There shall be a 4-inch (102 mm) porous layer of gravel, crushed stone or coarse sand placed under basement floor.

    R405.2

- A 6 millimeter-thick (0.15 mm) polyethylene moisture barrier is required over porous layer.

    R405.2

- Group I soils are exempt from drainage requirements.

    R405.2

- A sump required 24 inches (610 mm) in diameter or 20 inches square (0.0129 m^2).

    R405.2

WOOD FOUNDATION WALLS

WOOD FOUNDATION WALLS

- The sump is to extend 24 inches (610 mm) below the basement floor.

R405.2

- The drainage system shall discharge to daylight or approved sewer system.

R405.2

III. Insulating Concrete Form (ICF)

- Project documents are to bear the seal of the architect or engineer when not complying with Section R404.4 or ACI 318 or when required by state law.

R404.4

- Flat insulating concrete for wall systems shall have 5.5 inches (140 mm) minimum thickness, comply with Figure R611.3 and shall be reinforced in accordance with Tables R404.4(1), (2) or (3).

R404.4.2

- Waffle grid insulating concrete form wall systems shall have 6 inch (152 mm) minimum thickness for both horizontal and vertical cores, shall be reinforced in accordance with Table 404.4(4) and minimum core dimensions shall be per Figure R611.4 and Table R611.4(2).

R404.4.3

- Screen grid insulating concrete form wall systems shall have 6 inch (152 mm) minimum nominal thickness, horizontal and vertical wall systems, minimum core dimensions shall comply with Table R611.4(2) and Figure R611.5 and reinforcement of wall shall be per Table R404.4(5).

R404.4.4

A. Applicability limits for ICF foundation walls

- 60 feet (18 288 mm) maximum in plan dimension.
- 32 feet (9754 mm) maximum for floors.
- 40 feet (12 192 mm) maximum clear span for roofs.
- Two stories above grade, maximum 10 feet (3048 mm) each in height.
- 70 psf (3352 Pa) maximum ground snow load.
- SDC A, B or C only.

R404.4.1

B. Concrete material

- Maximum slump shall not be greater than 6 inches (152 mm).

    R404.4.5

- Maximum aggregate size is ¾ inch (19.1 mm). See exception.

    R404.4.5

C. Foam-plastic insulation

- Flame spread rating shall not exceed 75.

    R404.4.7

- Smoke-developed rating shall not exceed 450.

    R404.4.7

- A thermal barrier is required.

    R404.4.7

- Prevention of termite damage is required in areas of very heavy infestation.

    R404.4.7

- Thickness of ICF foundation walls shall not be less than wall supported.

    R404.4.8

- Height above finished ground shall have 4 inches (102 mm) minimum for masonry veneer, and 6 inches (152 mm) minimum elsewhere.

    R404.4.9

D. Reinforcing steel – General

- The minimum shall be Grade 40; increase spacing when using Grade 60.

    R404.4.6.1

- Rebar shall be placed no closer to outside face of wall than half the wall thickness.

    R404.4.6.1

- ICF remains in place; minimum concrete cover for rebar is ¾ inch (19.1 mm).

    R404.4.6.1

ICF FOUNDATION WALLS

COLUMNS AND UNDER-FLOOR SPACE

- Walls with vertical rebar shall have horizontal rebar.
- Walls to 8 feet (2438 mm) shall have one continuous No. 4, 48 inches (1219 mm) on center, and one bar within 12 inches (305 mm) of top of wall story.

R404.4.6.2

- Walls over 8 feet (2438 mm) shall have one continuous No. 4, 36 inches (914 mm) on center, and one bar within 12 inches (305 mm) of top of wall story.

R404.4.6.2

- Openings shall have no. 4 rebar within 12 inches (305 mm) on each side.

R404.4.6.3

IV. Columns

- Wood columns shall be protected against decay or constructed of approved pressure preservatively treated wood. See exceptions.

R407

- Steel columns shall have rust-inhibitive paint or be of a corrosion-resistant steel.

R407

- Columns shall be restrained at the bottom end. See exceptions.

R407

- Wood column shall not be less than 4 inches by 4 inches (102 mm by 102 mm).

R407

- Steel columns shall not be less than 3 inches (76 mm) in diameter.

R407

V. Under-Floor Space

- Ventilation is required through the foundation or exterior walls.

R408.1

- Minimum net area shall not be less than 1 square foot for each 150 square feet (.09 m^2 for each 14 m^2) of under floor area.

R408.1

- Ventilation openings shall be within 3 feet (914 mm) of each corner.

R408.2
- Openings shall be covered with approved materials. See exceptions.
- Minimum access opening is 18 inches by 24 inches (457 mm by 610 mm) through the floor, or is a minimum of 16 inches by 24 inches (407 mm by 610 mm) through the perimeter wall.

R408.3
- A 16-inch by 24-inch (407 mm by 610 mm) minimum areaway is required when any part of through-wall access is below grade.

R408.3

VI. Flooding

- Walls shall be provided with floor openings in areas prone to flooding.

R408.6
- Walls enclosing underfloor space shall be provided with flood openings.

R408.6
- The finished ground level of the underfloor space shall be equal to or higher than the outside finished ground level. See exceptions.

R408.6

WOOD FLOOR FRAMING

FLOORS

I. Wood Floor Framing

- Lumber shall bear a grade mark or certificate of inspection.

R502.1

- Decks shall be anchored to primary structure with a positive connection required or self-supporting.

R503.3.3

- Joist spans for sleeping areas shall comply with Table R502.3.1(1) and will not exceed 30 psf (1436 Pa).

R503.3.3

- Joist spans for other areas shall comply with Tables R502.3.1(2) and will not exceed 40 psf (1915 Pa).

R502.3.1

A. Floor cantilevers

- Cantilever spans shall not exceed depth of the wood floor joist.

R502.3.3

- Table R502.3.3(1) shall be used for bearing wall and roof only.

R503.3.3

- Cantilevers supporting exterior balcony are permitted per Table R502.3.3(2).

R502.3.3

B. Floor construction

- Joists under parallel bearing partitions to be sized to support load.

R502.4

- Bearing partitions perpendicular to joists shall not be offset from supporting girders, walls or partitions more than the joist depth unless sized for additional load.

R502.4

- Girder spans for interior bearing walls shall comply with Table R502.5(2).

R502.5

- Joist, beam or girder bearing on wood shall be a minimum of 1½ inches (38 mm); joist, beam or girder bearing on masonry or concrete not less than 3 inches (76 mm).

R502.6

19

- When balloon framing, the bearing is on 1-inch by 4-inch (25 mm by 102 mm) ribbon strip and nailed to an adjacent stud.

    R502

- Approved joist hangers shall be used.

    R502

- Minimum lap at bearing support shall be 3 inches (76 mm) and nailed with three 10d face nails.

    R502

- Wood or metal splice shall be used instead of a lap.

    R502

- Joists shall be framed into the side of a wood girder supported by framing anchors or ledger strip.

    R502

- Joists shall be supported laterally at ends.

    R502

- Joists shall be supported at intermediate support in SDC D_1 and D_2.

    R502

- 2-inch by 14-inch (51 mm by 356 mm) joists shall be mid-span blocked with 8 feet (2438 mm) maximum spacing.

    R502

C. Notching and boring of holes

- Notches shall not exceed D/6 of the member, shall not exceed D/3 in length and shall not be located in middle third of span.

    R502.8.1

- Notches at ends of member shall not exceed D/4.

    R502.8.1

- Holes bored or cut shall not exceed D/3.

    R502.8.1

- Holes shall not be closer than 2 inches (51 mm) to top or bottom of member, shall not be closer than 2 inches (51 mm) to other holes and shall not be closer than 2 inches (51 mm) to notch.

    R502.8.1

- Tension side of members 4 inches (102 mm) or more in thickness shall not be notched except at the ends.

    R502.8.1

WOOD FLOOR FRAMING

WOOD FLOOR FRAMING

- Trusses, laminated veneer lumber glue, laminated members or I-joists shall not be cut, notched or bored without the approval of a registered design professional.
R502.8.2

- Floor framing shall be nailed per Table R602.3(1).
R602.3

D. Framing around openings

- Positive connections are required for post and beam or girder construction.
R502.9

- Openings shall be framed with header and trimmer joists.
R502.10

- Openings from 4 feet (1219 mm) to 6 feet (1829 mm) shall double the header and trimmer joists.
R502.10

- Approved hanger is required for header joist exceeding 6 feet (1829 mm).
R502.10

- Approved hangers are required for tail joists over 12 feet (3658 mm) or use ledger strip that is no less than 2 inch by 2 inch (51 mm by 51 mm).
R502.10

E. Wood trusses

- Truss drawings shall be prepared by a registered design professional.
R502.11.1

- Trusses shall be braced per drawings on TP1, HIB.
R502.11.2

- Trusses shall not be cut, notched, spliced or altered without the approval of a registered design professional.
R502.11.3

- Additional loads for the truss (HVAC equipment, water heater, etc.) shall not be permitted without approval.
R502.11.3

- Truss drawings shall be delivered to and on the job site.
R502.11.3

21

F. Draftstopping

- Draftstopping is required when floor framing is constructed of truss-type open-web or perforated members, or if the ceiling is suspended under the floor framing.

    R502.12

- Maximum area is not to exceed 1,000 square feet (92.9 m^2).

    R502.12

- The space shall be divided into approximately equal areas.

    R502.12

- Approved materials shall be used for draftstopping.

    R502.12

- Fireblocking is required in wood-frame floor and floor ceiling assemblies.

    R602.8

II. Floor Sheathing

- Verify sheathing complies with Tables R503.1, R503.2.1.1(1) and R503.2.1.1(2) for minimum thickness for spacing; span rating; maximum span for roofs with edge support and without edge support; and maximum span for subfloor.

    R503.1

- End joints shall occur over supports unless end-matched lumber is used.

    R503.1.1

- Subflooring is omitted when joist spacing does not exceed 16 inches (406 mm) and when a 1-inch (25 mm) nominal tongue and groove wood strip is used.

    R503.1.1

A. Wood structural panel sheathing

- All panels shall be identified by grade mark or certificate of inspection.

    R503.2.1

- Subfloor and combined subfloor underlayment complies with Table R503.2.1.1(1) or R503.2.1.1(2).

    R503.2.2

- Maximum span complies with Table R503.2.1.1(1) or Table R503.2.1.1(2).

    R503.2.2

FLOOR SHEATHING

FLOOR SHEATHING

- Panels shall be attached to steel framing per Table R505.3.1(2).
  R503.2.3

B. Particleboard

- Particleboard shall have grade mark or certificate of inspection.
  R503.3.1
- Underlayment shall not be less than ¼ inch (6.4 mm).
  R503.3.2
- Underlayment shall conform to Type PBU.
  R503.3.2
- Particleboard shall be installed per manufacturers' recommendation and attached to framing per Table R602.3(1).
  R503.3.3

III. **Pressure Preservatively Treated Wood Floors (On Ground)**

- Unless special provision is made, wood basement floors shall be limited to where the depth of fill on the opposite sides is 2 feet (610 mm) or less.
  R504.1.1
- Joist wood in basement floors shall bear tightly against narrow face of studs, or directly against a band joist that bears on the studs.
  R504.1.2
- Plywood subfloor shall be continuous.
  R504.1.2
- Blocking shall be provided between joists.
  R504.1.2
- Resistance to uplift or restraint against buckling provided shall be when required.
  R504.1.3
- Area within foundation walls shall have all vegetation, top soil and foreign materials removed.
  R504.2
- Fill material shall be also free of vegetation and foreign material, as well as compacted.
  R504.2

- A 4-inch thick (102 mm) base of gravel is required over compacted earth.

    R504.2.1

- Gravel or crushed stone base shall have a maximum stone size of ½ inch (12.7 mm).

    R504.2.1

- Moisture barrier with laps is required.

    R504.2.2

- Moisture barrier shall not exceed beneath exterior wall footing plates.

    R504.2.2

- Sleepers, joists, blocking and plywood subfloor shall be pressure preservatively treated.

    R504

IV. Steel Floor Framing

- Floor framing shall be straight and free of defects.

    R505.1

- Steel floor framing is controlled in buildings greater than 60 feet (18 288 mm) in length perpendicular to joists.

    R505.1.1

- Floor framing shall not be greater than 36 feet (10 973 mm) in width parallel to joist spans.

    R505.1.1

- Floor framing shall not be greater than two stories in height.

    R505.1.1

- Stories shall not exceed 10 feet (3048 mm) in height.

    R505.1.1

- Locations are limited to sites subjected to maximum wind speed of 110 mph (209 km/hr).

    R505.1.1

- SDC A, B and C only.

    R505.1.1

- Floor framing limited to a maximum ground snow load of 70 psf (3352 Pa).

    R505.1.1

WOOD FLOORS ON GROUND

STEEL FLOOR FRAMING

A. In-line framing

- Floor joists shall be located directly in line with load-bearing studs. There shall be a maximum tolerance ¾ inch (19.1 mm) center line to center line.

R505.1.2

B. Structural framing

- Load-bearing floor members shall comply with Figure R505.2.1(1) and Tables R505.2(1).

R505.2

- Tracks shall comply with Figure R505.2(2) and shall have minimum flange width of 1⅛ inches (32 mm).

R505.2

- The maximum inside bend radius shall be $^3/_{32}$ inch (2.4 mm) or twice uncoated steel thickness.

R505.2

- Holes shall comply with Figure R505.2(3) and are permitted only along centerline of web and patched per Section R505.3.6.

R505.2

- Load-bearing steel shall be identified, have corrosion protection and be fastened per Section R505.2.4 and Table R505.2.4.

R505.2

C. Cold-formed steel floors

- Floors shall comply with Section R505.3 and Figure R505.3.

R404.3.1

- Floors shall be anchored per Table R505.3.1(1) and Figures R404.3.1(1), (2), (3), (4), (5) and (6), and shall be supported by interior load-bearing walls per Figure R505.3.1(7).

R404.3.1

- Floors shall have lapped steel per Figure R505.3.1(8).

R404.3.1

- Floors shall be fastened to other framing members per Table R404.3.1(2).

R404.3.1

D. Allowable joist spans

- Joist spans shall not exceed limits of Table R505.3.2.

R505.3.2

25

- The minimum bearing of a joist span shall be $1^1/_2$ inches (38 mm).

    R505.3.2

- Joist spans shall have interior bearing supports located within 2 feet (610 mm) of mid span of continuous joists.

    R505.3.2

- Joist spans shall have bearing stiffeners installed at bearing locations.

    R505.3.2

E. Joist bracing

- Top flanges shall be laterally braced.

    R505.3.3

- Bottom flanges shall be laterally braced when joists have spans that exceed 12 feet (3658 mm).

    R505.3.3

F. Bearing stiffeners

- Stiffeners shall be installed at all bearing locations.

    R505.3.5

- Bearing stiffeners shall be fabricated from a minimum 33 millimeter C-section or 43 millimeter back section.

    R505.3.4

- Four No. 8 screws are required for fasteners.

    R505.3.4

- Stiffeners are required to extend full depth and be installed on either side.

    R505.3.4

- Flanges and lips of load-bearing members shall not be cut or notched.

    R505.3.5

G. Hole patching

- Hole patching is required when the hole is closer than 10 inches (254 mm) from the edge of the hole to the bearing surface.

- The patch shall be a solid steel plate, C-section or track section.

    R505.3.6

STEEL FLOOR FRAMING

STEEL FLOOR FRAMING

- The patch shall extend a minimum of 1 inch (25 mm) beyond all edges of the hole.

R505.3.6

- No. 8 screws shall be spaced no greater than 1 inch (25 mm) center to center of edges, with a minimum edge distance of $1/2$ inch (12.7 mm).

R505.3.6

H. Floor cantilevers

- Cantilevers shall not exceed 24 inches (610 mm).

R505.3.7

- A minimum 6-foot (1830 mm) back span if required.

R505.3.7

- Double joist members shall be used, fastened web-to-web.
- Built-up floor framing is permitted in lieu of web-to-web double joist.

R505.3.7

- Cantilevers shall be permitted on the second floor of a two-story building or the first floor of a one-story building.

R505.3.7

- Joists and other structural members shall not be spliced; however, tracks shall be spliced per Figure R505.3.8.

R505.3.8

I. Framing of openings

- Header and trimmer joists are required.

R505.3.9

- The maximum span of the header joist shall not exceed 8 feet (2438 mm), which will be fabricated from track and joist sections, the same size as floor joists.
- Each header joist shall be connected to trimmers with minimum of four 2-inch by 2-inch (51 mm by 51 mm) clip angles with No. 8 screws evenly spaced.

R505.3.9

- Clip angles are required to have a thickness no less than the floor joist.

R505.3.9

V. Concrete Floors (On Ground)

- Minimum thickness of floors shall be $3^1/_2$ inches (89 mm).
  R506.1
- All vegetation, top soil and foreign material shall be removed.
  R506.2
- Fill shall also be free of vegetation and foreign material, as well as compacted.
  R506.2.1
- Fill shall not exceed 24 inches (610 mm) for clean sand or gravel and 8 inches (203 mm) for earth.
  R506.2.1
- Base course required unless slab is installed on Group I soils.
  R506.2.2
- Vapor retarder shall be placed between floor slab and base course or subgrade. See exception.
  R506.2.3

CONCRETE FLOORS ON GROUND

LOCATION ON LOT

FRAMING INSPECTION

After the wood framing, rough electrical, rough plumbing and rough mechanical portions of the project have been completed, the code requires a framing inspection. The following are those provisions that should be included in the inspection process at an early stage. It should be noted that a few of these, such as glass and glazing, handrails and guardrails, will appear on the final inspection list also.

I. Location On Lot

- One-hour fire-resistive rating required for exterior walls with a fire separation distance of less than 3 feet (914 mm). Walls are to be rated from both sides.

R302.1

A. Projection from exterior walls

- Projections are not to extend within 2 feet (610 mm) of fire separation line.

R302.1

- Openings are not permitted in walls with less than 3 feet (914 mm) separation. See exceptions.

R302.2

II. Light, Ventilation and Heating

- Natural light shall not be less than 8 percent of the floor area. See exceptions.

R303.1

- Natural ventilation shall be 4 percent of the floor area. See exceptions.

R303.1

A. Adjoining rooms

- 10 percent of the floor area of an interior room is required for opening, but no less then 25 square feet (2.32 m²).

R303.2

- At least one-half of common wall is open and obstructed. See exceptions.

R303.2

B. Bathrooms

- Natural light shall not be less than 3 square feet (.28 m²)—one-half openable for ventilation. See exception.

R303.3

- A minimum of 50 cubic feet per minute (cfm) (.02 m^3/s) for intermittent ventilation or 20 cfm (.009 m^3/s) for continuous ventilation is required.

  R303.3

- Ventilation air from space shall be exhausted directly outside.

  R303.3

C. Opening location

- Mechanical and gravity outside air intake openings shall be a minimum of 10 feet (3048 mm) from any vent, chimney, plumbing vent, street, alley, parking lot or loading dock unless it is 2 feet (610 mm) below the source.

  R303.4

- Exhaust from dwelling units, toilet rooms, bathrooms and kitchens are not considered hazardous or noxious.

  R303.4

- Outside exhaust openings located so as not to create a nuisance; exhaust air shall not be directed onto walkways.

  R303.4

- Outside openings shall be protected by corrosion-resistant screens, louvers or grills with a minimum opening size of ¼ inch (6.4 mm), and a maximum of ½ inch (12.7 mm); and protected against local weather conditions.

  R303.5

- Outdoor openings shall be protected as required for exterior wall openings.

  R303.5

D. Stairway illumination

- Interior and exterior stairways are required to be provided with means to illuminate stairs, landings and treads.

  R303.6

- Exterior stairs are to be provided with a light source at the top landing. See exception.

  R303.6

E. Required glazed openings

- Required openings shall open directly onto the street or public alley, yard or court.

  R303.7

LIGHT AND VENTILATION

ROOM HEIGHTS AND AREAS

- Required glazed openings may face onto roofed porch where porch abuts street, yard or court: the long side of the porch shall be a minimum 65-percent open, and the ceiling height shall not exceed 7 feet (2134 mm).

R303.5

III. Minimum Room Areas

- There shall be at least one room with 120-square-feet (11.2 m²) gross floor area.

R304.1

- Other habitable rooms shall not be less than 70 square feet (6.5 m²).

R304.2

- The kitchen shall not be less than 50-square-feet (4.64 m²) gross floor area.

- The minimum horizontal dimension, except in kitchen, shall not be less than 7 feet (2134 mm).

R304.4

- Portions of a room with a sloped ceiling less than 5 feet (1524 mm) or a furred ceiling less than 7 feet (2134 mm) shall not be considered as a portion of the required area.

R304.4

IV. Ceiling Height

- Minimum ceiling height in habitable areas shall be 7 feet (2134 mm). See exceptions.

R305

V. Sanitation

- Every dwelling unit shall have a:
  1. Water closet.
  2. Lavatory.
  3. Bathtub or shower.
  4. Kitchen area.
  5. Kitchen sink.
  6. Connection to sanitary sewer or private sewage disposal system.

7. Approved water supply
  8. Hot and cold water.

R306

VI. Toilet, Bath and Shower Spaces

- Fixtures shall be spaced a minimum of:
    1. 4 inches (102 mm) from lavatory to wall.
    2. 21 inches (533 mm) in front of lavatory.
    3. 21 inches (533 mm) in front of water closet.
    4. 2 inches (51 mm) between lavatory and bathtub.
    5. 4 inches (102 mm) between water closet and lavatory.
    6. 4 inches (102 mm) between lavatories.
    7. 15 inches (381 mm) from center line of water closet to wall or bathtub.
    8. 900 square inches (.58 m^2) for the shower, 30 inches (762 mm) minimum in any direction.
    9. 24 inches (610 mm) in front of the shower.

R307

VII. Glazing

- Each pane of glazing installed in a hazardous location shall be labeled as safety type. See exceptions to approval by the building official.

R308.1

- Glass in louvered windows or jalousies shall not be less than $3/16$-inch (4.76 mm) thick or longer than 48 inches (1219 mm). Exposed edges shall be smooth.

R308.2

- Wire glass with exposed wire shall not be used in jalousies or louvered windows.

R308.2.1

- Human impact/hazardous locations:
    1. Swinging doors, except jalousies.
    2. Fixed and sliding panels of sliding doors and closet door assemblies.
    3. Storm doors.
    4. Unframed swinging doors.

GLAZING

GLAZING

5. Doors and enclosures for hot tubs, whirlpools, saunas, steam rooms, bathtubs and showers; any part of building wall enclosing these compartments with a bottom edge less than 60 inches (1524 mm) above the floor.

6. Individual fixed or operable panel adjacent to a door within 24 inches (610 mm) of arc and bottom edge that is less than 60 inches (1524 mm) above the floor.

7. Individual fixed or operable panel other than those in Items 5 and 6 above, that meet all of the following:

    a) Area is greater than 9 square feet (0.836 m^2);

    b) Bottom edge is less than 18 inches (457 mm) above floor;

    c) Top edge is greater than 36 inches (914 mm) above floor; and

    d) Walking surfaces within 36 inches (914 mm) horizontally of glazing.

8. All railings including structural baluster panels and nonstructural in-fill panels.

9. Walls and fences enclosing indoor and outdoor swimming pools, hot tubs and spas where bottom edge on pool or spa side is less than 60 inches (1524 mm) above walking surface and within 60 inches (1524 mm) horizontally to water edge.

10. Glazing adjacent to stairways, landings and ramps within 36 inches (914 mm) horizontally of walking surface, with glass less than 60 inches above plane of adjacent walking surface.

11. Walls enclosing stairway landings or within 60 inches (1524 mm) of top or bottom of the stairs when bottom edge of glazing is less than 60 inches (1524 mm) above walking surface. See exceptions.

R308.4

VIII. Garages and Carports

- Openings are not permitted from the garage directly into a room used for sleeping purposes.

    R309.1

- Doors shall be solid wood a minimum of $1^3/_8$ inches (35 mm) in thickness; solid or honeycomb core steel doors a minimum of $1^3/_8$ inches (35 mm) in thickness; or 20-minute, fire-rated door.

    R309.1

- Duct penetration, walls or ceiling shall have No. 26 gage steel sheet or other approved material—no openings into garage.

    R309.1.1

- Separation from residence and attic shall have ½-inch (12.7 mm) gypsum board applied to garage side.

    R309.2

- A $^5/_8$-inch (15.9 mm) Type X gypsum board or equivalent is required between the garage and habitable space above the garage.

    R309.2

- A ½-inch (12.7 mm) gypsum board or equivalent is required on a structure supporting horizontal separation.

    R309.2

- Floors shall be approved for noncombustible materials. An asphalt permit is required for carports at ground level.

    R309.2

- Garage floors shall be at or above flood elevation or used only for storage and parking.

    R309.3

IX. Emergency Escape and Rescue Openings

NOTE: Openings are required for all sleeping rooms and basements with habitable space.

- Every sleeping room in basements is required to have an escape/rescue opening; however, this is not required in other areas of the basement.

    R310.1

- Sill height is not to exceed 44 inches (1118 mm) above floor.

    R310.1

GARAGES AND CARPORTS

MEANS OF EGRESS

- A 5.7-square-foot (0.530 m²) net clear minimum opening is required. See exception.

R310.1.1

- A 24-inch (610 mm) net clear height is required in openable portion.

R310.1.2

- A 20-inch (508 mm) net clear width is required in openable portion.

R310.1.3

A. Window wells

- Wells shall have 9 square feet (0.84 m²) minimum horizontal area.

R310.2

- Wells shall have 36 inches (914 mm) minimum horizontal projection and width.

R310.2

- Ladder or steps are permitted to encroach 6 inches (152 mm) in required dimension.

R310.2.1

- Ladder or steps are required when vertical depth exceeds 44 inches (1118 mm).

R310.2.1

- Bulkhead enclosures shall provide direct access to the basement.

R310.3

- Approved bars, grills, covers or screens shall be used.

R310.4

X. **Means of Egress**

- Stairways, ramps, exterior exit balconies, hallways and doors shall comply with code.

R311.1

- Required exterior elements shall be positively anchored to the primary structure to resist vertical and lateral forces.

R311.2.1

- Enclosed accessible space under stairs shall be protected on enclosed side with a ½-inch (12.7 mm) gypsum board.

R311.2.2

- Hallways shall have 36 inches (914 mm) minimum width.
  R311.3

- Required exit door shall be side-hinged swinging, 6 feet 8 inches (2032 mm) in height and 3 feet (914 mm) in width.
  R311.4.1

- Required exit door directly to exterior is not permitted to travel through the garage; access to habitable areas not meeting this requirement shall be by a ramp or stairway.
  R311.4.1

- Floor or landing is required on each side of the exterior door. See exception.
  R311.4.3

- Landing or floor shall be a maximum 1½ inches (38 mm) lower than the top of the threshold; 7¾ inches (196 mm) is permitted at doors that are not required exit doors.
  R311.4.3

- Width of landing shall not be less than the door served; it shall be 36 inches (914 mm) minimum in direction of travel.
  R311.4.3

- Egress doors shall be readily openable from the inside without the use of keys or special knowledge or effort.
  R311.4.4

A. Stairways

- Stairways shall have a minimum 36-inch (914 mm) width.
  R311.5.1

- Maximum riser height of stairways shall be 7¾ inches (196 mm), and a minimum tread of 10 inches (254 mm). The maximum variation shall not exceed $3/8$ inch (9.5 mm).
  R311.5.3.1

- Handrails shall not project more than 4.5 inches (114 mm) on each side.
  R311.5.1

- Minimum headroom in stairways shall be 6 feet 8 inches (2032 mm).
  R311.5.2

- A floor or landing is required at the top and bottom of each stairway. See exception.
  R311.5.4

STAIRWAYS

STAIRWAYS

- The maximum vertical rise shall be 12 feet (3658 mm) between landings.

R311.5.4

- The walking surface shall be no steeper than 1:48 (2-percent slope).

R311.5.5

1. Winders
   - The minimum width at the narrower point of winder shall be 6 inches (152 mm).

R311.5.3.2

   - A 10-inch (254 mm) minimum width is required at point 12 inches (305 mm) from the narrower side.

R311.5.3.2

2. Spiral stairs
   - Spiral stairs shall have a minimum width of 26 inches (660 mm).
   - A 7⅞ inch (190 mm) minimum width is required at point 12 inches (305 mm) from the narrow edge.

R311.5.8.1

   - Stairs shall have a 9½-inch (241 mm) maximum rise.

R311.3.8.1

   - Stairways shall have 6-feet 6-inch (1982 mm) minimum headroom.

R311.5.8.1

3. Circular stairways
   - An 11-inch (279 mm) minimum width is required at point 12 inches (305 mm) from the narrower side.

R311.5.8.1

   - A 6-inch (152 mm) minimum tread is required at any point.

R311.5.8.1

4. Bulkhead stairways are exempt when enclosed with hinged doors or other approved means.

R311.5.8.2

B. Handrails
   - Required for stairs with four or more risers.

R311.5.6.1

   - Minimum height of handrails shall be 34 inches (864 mm).

R311.5.6.1

- Maximum height of handrails shall be 38 inches (965 mm).
  R311.5.6.1
- Height is measured vertically above nosing of tread.
  R311.5.6.1
- Handrails are provided for a continuous full length of stairs from directly above top riser to directly above lowest riser.
  R311.5.6
- Ends shall terminate to wall or newel post.
  R311.5.6.2
- Interruption of handrail is permitted by a newel post at a turn.
  R311.5.6.2
- Volute, turnout or starting easing is permitted over the lowest tread.
  R311.5.6.2
- A minimum space less than 1½ inches (38 mm) between wall and handrails is required.
  R311.5.6.2

C. Handrail grip size

TYPE I

- Circular cross sections shall be a minimum 1¼ inches (32 mm) and a maximum 2 inches (51 mm).
  R311.5.6.3
- Noncircular cross sections shall have a perimeter that is a minimum 4 inches (102 mm), maximum 6¼ inches (160 mm), and a maximum cross-sectional area that is 2¼ inches (57 mm).
  R311.5.6.3

TYPE II

- A perimeter exceeding 6¼ inches (160 mm) requires a graspable finger recess area on both sides.
  R311.5.6.3

D. Ramps

- Ramps shall have a maximum slope of 1:8 (12.5 percent slope).
  R311.6.1
- Landings shall be a minimum 3 feet by 3 feet (914 mm by 914 mm).
  R311.6.2

RAMPS

GUARDS AND SMOKE ALARMS

- Landings are required at:
  1. Top and bottom of stairs.
  2. Where doors open onto ramps.
  3. Change of direction.

R311.6.2

- Handrails are required on at least one side when ramp exceeds 1:12 (8.33-percent slope).

R311.6.3

- Height of handrail shall not be less than 34 inches (864 mm) or more than 38 inches (965 mm) above the finished surface.

R311.6.3.1

- Handrails shall be continuous, ends shall be returned, and there shall be a minimum 1½-inch (38 mm) clearance between wall and handrail.

R311.6.3.3

XI. Guards

- Guards are required for porches, balconies or raised floor surfaces located more than 30 inches (762 mm) above floor or grade below; guard height shall be a minimum of 36 inches (914 mm).

R312.1

- Guard height shall be a minimum of 34 inches (864 mm) on open sides of stairs more than 30 inches (762 mm) above floor or grade below.

R312.1

- Guards shall have a maximum opening such that a 4-inch (102 mm) sphere cannot pass through.

R312.2

- A maximum 6-inch (152 mm) opening is permitted at a triangular opening formed by a riser, tread and bottom rail of a guard.

R316

XII. Smoke Alarms

- Single- and multiple-station smoke alarms shall be installed:
  1. In each bedroom;
  2. Outside each separate sleeping area in the immediate vicinity of the bedrooms; and

3. On each story, including basements, but not including crawl spaces and uninhabitable attics.

   R313.1

- Interconnection is required between two or more alarms.

  R313.1

- Primary power from building wiring is required in new construction, including remodeling or additions.

  R313.2

- Alarms shall be hardwired where required in existing dwellings whenever attic, crawl space or basement provides access for hardwiring and interconnection, or where work is being done that causes removal of interior wall or ceiling finish.

  R313.1.1

- Wiring is to be permanent and without a disconnection switch other than that required for overcurrent protection.

  R313.2

XIII. Dwelling Unit Separation

- Dwelling units in two-family dwellings shall be separated by no less than 1-hour wall and/or floor assemblies.

  R317.1

- Fire-resistant separation shall extend to and be tight against exterior wall and extend to underside of roof sheathing.

  R317.1

- Vertical supports of horizontal separations shall have an equal fire-resistance rating.

  R317.1

- Townhouse separations to consist of two 1-hour fire-rated walls.

- A common 2-hour wall is permitted for townhouse construction; walls shall not contain plumbing or mechanical systems, ducts or vents. Electrical installation is permitted when complying with the *National Electrical Code.*

  R317.2

- Common walls shall be continuous from foundation to underside of roof sheathing, deck or slab, and shall extend the full length of common wall including walls extending through/separating accessory structures.

  R317.2.1

PROTECTION AGAINST DECAY

- Parapets, when required, shall be rated the same as common walls.

R317.2.3

- Individual townhouses are to be structurally independent. See exceptions.

R317.2.4

- Through penetration or membrane penetration protection is required for penetrations of fire-resistance-rated walls or floors. See exception.

R317.3

XIV. Moisture Vapor Retarders

- Vapor retarders shall be installed in all framed walls, floors and roof/ceilings comprising the building's thermal envelope. See exceptions.

R318.1

XV. Protection Against Decay

- Protection against decay with pressure-treated lumber or heartwood of redwood, black locust or cedar shall be used in the following locations:

1. Floor systems when joists are within 18 inches (457 mm) or girders are within 12 inches (305 mm) of ground.
2. All wood framing members on concrete or masonry exterior walls that extend less than 8 inches (203 mm) above ground.
3. Sills or sleepers on concrete or masonry slabs, unless separated by impervious moisture barrier.
4. Ends of girders entering exterior masonry or concrete walls with clearances less than ½ inch (12.7 mm) on top, sides and ends.
5. Wood siding, sheathing and wall framing with less than 6 inches (152 mm) clearance from the ground.
6. Wood structural members of weather exposed permeable floors.
7. Wood furring strips attached to below-grade concrete, unless vapor retarder is installed.

R319.1

- Wood in continual direct contact with ground shall be approved pressure preservatively treated wood.

    R319.1.1

- Weather exposed wood in specific geographical areas shall be approved.

    R319.1.2

- Posts, columns and poles embedded in concrete shall be approved.

    R319.1.3

A. Wood columns

- Approved wood of natural decay resistance or approved pressure preservatively treated wood shall be used for wood columns. See exceptions.

    R319.1.4

- A grade/quality mark is required.

    R319.2

- Fasteners for pressure treated lumber, except for ½ inch (12.7 mm) or greater steel bolts, shall be hot-dipped galvanized steel, stainless steel, silicon bronze or copper.

    R319.3

XVI. Protection Against Termites

- Protection from termites shall be by one or more of the following methods:

    1. Chemical soil treatment.
    2. Pressure-treated wood.
    3. Naturally termite-resistant wood.
    4. Physical barriers.

    R320.1

- Lumber and plywood shall have a quality mark.

    R320.1.1

- Field cuts, notches and drilled holes of pressure-treated wood shall be retreated.

    R320.3.1

- Expanded and extruded polystyrene and other foam plastics shall be limited.

    R320.4

PROTECTION AGAINST TERMITES

FLOOD-RESISTANT CONSTRUCTION

XVII. Flood-Resistant Construction

- All buildings and structures erected in areas prone to flooding shall be constructed and elevated per Section R323.
R323.1

- Buildings in floodways shall comply with the IBC.
R323.1

- Structures shall be constructed to minimize flood damage.
R323.1.1

- Design flood elevation shall be a 100-year storm peak elevation.
R323.1.3

- Use of lowest floor shall be limited to vehicle parking, storage or access.
R323.1.4

- Mechanical, electrical and plumbing systems shall be protected.
R323.1.5

- Water supply shall be protected.
R323.1.6

- Flood-resistant building materials shall be used.
R323.1.7

- Manufactured housing shall be certified by a registered design professional.
R323.1.8

- Flood-hazard areas shall be identified.
R323.2

- The use of enclosed areas below design flood elevation shall be limited to the parking of vehicles, building access and storage.
R323.2.2, R323.3.5

- Buildings in coastal high-hazard areas shall comply with Sections R323.3.1 through R323.3.5.
R323.3

- Special flood requirements shall be used for walls below design flood elevation, but shall not be a part of the structural support of building.
R323.3.4

- A registered design professional is required for the design and methods of construction.

    R323.3.6

XVIII. Miscellaneous

- Site address shall be visible and legible from street or road fronting property.

    R321.1

- Where townhouse contains four or more dwelling units, accessibility provisions of the IBC for Group R-3 occupancy are applicable.

    R322.1

WOOD WALL FRAMING

WALL CONSTRUCTION

I. **Wood Wall Framing**

- Load-bearing dimension lumber shall have a grade mark or certificate of inspection.

R602.1

- Approved end-jointed lumber is permitted to be used interchangeably with solid-sawn members of the same species.

R602.1.1

- Glued laminated timbers shall comply with AITC A190.1 and ASTM D 3737.

R602.1.2.

- Studs shall be a minimum No. 3, standard or stud grade lumber.

R602.2

- Bearing studs not supporting floors and nonbearing studs may be utility grade.

R602.2

A. Studs spacing; bearing walls

- Studs not more than 10 feet (3048 mm) in height to comply with Table R602.3(5).

R602.3.1

- Studs more than 10 feet (3048 mm) in height to comply with Table R602.3.1.

R602.3.1

- A double top-plate is required; the offset for the end joints shall be no less than 24 inches (610 mm). See exceptions for use of single top plate.

R602.3.2

- Studs spaced 24 inches (610 mm) on center shall be within 5 inches (127 mm) of joists trusses or rafters. See exceptions.

R602.3.3

- Studs shall have full bearing on plate or sill at least equal to the width of the studs.

R602.3.4

- Interior load-bearing walls shall be constructed, framed and blocked as for exterior walls.

R602.4

45

B. Interior nonbearing walls
- Studs shall be 2 inch by 3 inch (51 mm by 76 mm) minimum, and 24 inches (610 mm) on center minimum.
  R602.5
- 2-inch by 4-inch (51 mm by 102 mm) flat studs at 16 inches (406 mm) may be used when not a part of a braced wall line.
  R602.5
- Fireblocking is required per Section R602.8.
  R602.5

C. Drilling and notching studs
- A 25-percent maximum cut or notch is permitted for bearing or exterior studs.
  R602.6
- A 40-percent maximum cut or notch is permitted for nonbearing studs.
  R602.6
- Drilled holes shall not exceed 40 percent of a single stud width, and the edge shall be no closer than $^5/_8$ inch (15.9 mm) to the edge of the stud.
  R602.6
- A notch and hole shall not be in the same section.
  R602.6
- Exterior or load-bearing walls with plates cut, drilled or notched more than 50 percent of the width of the stud shall have:
  1. Galvanized metal tie 16 gage and 1½ inches (38 mm) wide fastened to each plate.
  2. Minimum of eight 16d nails on each side or equivalent.
  R602.6.1

D. Headers
- Verify Table R502.5(1) for girder and header spans for exterior bearing walls.
  R602.7
- Verify Table R502.5(2) for girder and header spans for interior bearing walls.
  R602.7
- Wood structural panel box headers shall be constructed per Figure R602.7.2 and Table R602.7.2.
  R602.7.1

WOOD WALL FRAMING

FIREBLOCKING

- A single flat 2-inch by 4-inch (51 mm by 102 mm) header may be used in nonbearing walls: header shall be a maximum 8 feet (2438 mm) in width and vertical distance to parallel nailing surface not more than 24 inches (610 mm).

R602.7.2

E. Fireblocking

- Fireblocking is required to cut off all concealed draft openings—vertical and horizontal—and form effective fire barriers between stories, top story and roof space and in the following locations:
    1. Concealed spaces in stud walls and partitions, including parallel rows or staggered studs, at minimum 10-foot (3048 mm) intervals.
    2. Interconnections between vertical and horizontal spaces such as soffits, drop ceilings and cove ceilings.
    3. Concealed spaces between stair stringers, at top and bottom of run.
    4. Penetrations of top, sole or sill plate: use approved material to resist flame.
    5. Chimneys and fireplace shafts.
    6. Cornices of two-family dwellings at dwelling separation.

R602.8

- Materials for fireblocking shall be:
    1. 2-inch (51 mm) nominal lumber.
    2. Two 1-inch (25 mm) nominal lumber with broken lap joints.
    3. $^{23}/_{32}$-inch (19.8 mm) wood structural panel.
    4. ¾-inch (19.1 mm) particleboard with joists backed.
    5. ½-inch (12.7 mm) gypsum board.
    6. ¼-inch cement-based mill board.
    7. Batts or blankets or loose fill insulation with specific limitations and requirements.
    8. Unfaced fiberglass batt insulation per installation instructions.

R602.8.1

F. Cripple walls

- Cripple walls shall be:
    1. Minimum of same size as studs above;
    2. Considered additional story when greater than 4 feet (1219 mm) in height;
    3. Sheathed at least one side with wood structural panel, or solid blocked; and

4. Supported on continuous foundations.

R602.9

G. Wall bracing—exterior walls

- Walls of buildings located in SDC D_1 and D_2 shall be constructed in accordance with Sections R602.10.9, R602.10.11 and R602.11.

R602.10

- Amount and location of braced wall lines shall comply with methods per Table R602.10.3.

R602.10.1

- Wall bracing shall begin no more than 12½ feet (3810 mm) from each end of a braced wall line.

R602.10.1

- Wall offsets out-of-plane shall be 4 feet (1219 mm) maximum, while total out-of-plane offset dimension in any wall line shall be no more than 8 feet (2438 mm).

R602.10.1

- A designed collector is required when bracing begins more than 12 feet (3658 mm) from each end of braced wall line.

R602.10.1

  1. Braced wall-line spacing
     - Maximum braced wall-line spacing shall be 35 feet (10 668 mm) on center both ways in each story. See exceptions.

R602.10.1.1

H. Cripple wall bracing

- In other than SDC D_2, wall shall be braced per Table R602.10.1. See exceptions.

R602.10.2.1

- In SDC D_2, cripple walls shall comply with Table R602.10.1.

R602.10.2.2

  1. Redesignation of cripple walls
     - Cripple walls, in any SDC, may be treated as first story walls for purposes of determining wall bracing.

R602.10.2.3

I. Braced wall panel construction methods

  1. Nominal 1-inch by 4-inch (25.4 mm by 102 mm) diagonal brace shall be let in to studs and top and bottom plates; shall be angled at 60 degrees to 45 degrees.

WALL BRACING

BRACED WALL PANELS

2. Minimum $^5/_8$-inch-thick (15.9 mm) wood boards shall be applied diagonally.
3. Minimum $^5/_{16}$-inch-thick (7.9 mm) minimum structural wood sheathing shall be used.
4. Minimum ½-inch-thick (12.7 mm) or $^{25}/_{32}$-inch-thick (19.8 mm) structural fiberboard sheathing shall be used.
5. Minimum ½-inch-thick (12.7 mm) gypsum wall board shall be used.
6. Particleboard shall be installed per Table R602.3(4).
7. Portland cement plaster shall be installed per Section R703.6.
8. Hardboard siding shall be installed per Table R703.4.

R602.10.3
- Minimum length of braced panels shall be 48 inches (1219 mm) minimum for Methods 2, 3, 4, 6 and 7 above, and 96 inches (2438 mm) minimum for Method 5 unless applied to both faces. See exceptions.

R602.10.4

J. Continuous structural panel sheathing
- Method 3 above will apply, length per Table R602.10.5, for exterior walls and interior braced wall lines.

R602.10.5
- Corners shall be per Figure R602.10.5.

R602.10.5
- Method 3 shall be multiplied by a factor of 0.9 for amounts from Table R602.10.3 with maximum opening height not exceeding 85 percent of wall height, or a factor of 0.8 when opening does not exceed 67 percent of wall height.

R602.10.5

K. Alternate braced wall panels
- Alternate braced wall panels shall replace each 4 feet of braced wall panel when in accordance with 1 or 2 below:

1. One-story building
- Each panel shall be 2 feet 8 inches (813 mm) minimum and 10-foot (3048 mm) maximum height.
- Minimum $^3/_8$-inch (9.5 mm) wood structural panel sheathing is required.
- Wall anchorage shall be per Figure R403.1(1).
- Anchor bolts shall be at quarter points.

- A tie down shall be at each end with an uplift capacity of 1,800 pounds (816.5 kg) minimum.
- Panel shall have continuous reinforcement, with a maximum of one No. 4 rebar top and bottom.

R602.10.6

2. Two-story building (same as one-story building with the following exceptions):
   - Minimum $^3/_8$-inch (99.5 mm) wood structural panels are required on each face.
   - Anchor bolts shall be at one-fifth points.
   - Tie downs shall have a minimum uplift capacity of 3,000 pounds (1361 kg).

R602.10.6

- Vertical panel joints shall occur over studs.

R602.10.7

- Horizontal panel joints shall occur over 1½-inch (38 mm) blocking. See exception.

R602.10.7

L. Connections

- Braced wall panel sole plates shall comply with Table R602.3(1) for fasteners to framing.

R602.10.8

- Sills shall be fastened to the foundation or slab per Sections R403.1.6 and R602.11.

R602.10.8

- Blocking is required under and in line with braced wall panels where joists are perpendicular to the braced wall.

R602.10.8

M. Interior braced wall support

- For a one-story building, the SDC D_2 shall have continuous foundations at intervals not exceeding 50 feet (15 240 mm) for braced wall lines.

R602.10.9

- For a two-story building, the SDC D_2 shall have all interior braced wall lines supported on continuous footings. See exceptions.

R602.10.9

BRACED WALL PANELS

WALL BRACING

N. Bracing in SDC D$_1$ and D$_2$

- Exterior and interior braced wall lines are required for SDC D$_1$ and D$_2$.
R602.10.11

- Spacing between wall lines shall not exceed 25 feet (7620 mm) on center. See exception.
R602.10.11

- The multiplier (Table R602.10.11) applies to walls spaced greater or less than 25 feet (7620 mm) apart.
R602.10.11

- A braced wall panel is required at both ends of an exterior braced wall line. See exceptions.
R602.10.11

- A designed collector is required when bracing is not located at each end or is located more than 8 feet (2438 mm) from ends of wall line per exception.
R602.10.11

1. Cripple wall bracing

- Exterior cripple wall bracing shall be one and one-half times the required length when continuous foundation is omitted.
R602.10.11

- Where bracing Method 3 cannot provide additional length, fasteners shall be spaced 4 inches (102 mm) on center.
R602.10.11

- Adhesive attachment of wall sheathing shall not be applied in SDC C, D$_1$ and D$_2$.
R602.10.11

O. Framing and connections for SDC D$_1$ and D$_2$

- Sills are to be anchored per Sections R403.1.6 and R602.11.
R602.11

- Plate washers, minimum $^1/_4$ inch by 3 inches by 3 inches (6.4 mm by 76 mm by 76 mm), shall be used for buildings in SDC D$_1$ and D$_2$ and townhouses in SDC C.
R602.11.1

51

- Interior braced wall panels shall be fastened per Table R602.3(1), with 8d nails 6 inches (150 mm) on center, parallel floor joists shall be toe nailed to the top plate and eight 16d nails on each side of top plate splice.

    R602.11.2

P. Stepped foundations

- Figure R602.11.3 applies when height of panels varies more than 4 feet (1220 mm).

    R602.11.3

- The wall is considered braced when the lowest floor framing rests directly on the foundation no less than 8 feet (2440 mm) long.

    R602.11.3

- Anchor bolts to be located a maximum of 1 foot and 3 feet (305 mm and 914 mm) from step in foundation.

    R602.11.3

- Bracing per story is required when a cripple wall occurs between the top of the foundation at the lowest floor framing.

    R602.11.3

- Section R602.11.1 applies only when the bottom of the foundation is stepped and the lowest floor is framed to sill that is bolted to the foundation.

    R602.11.3

II. Steel Wall Framing

- Elements shall be straight and free of any defects.

    R603.1

A. Applicability limits

- 60 feet (18 288 mm) in maximum length perpendicular to joist or truss span.

    R603.1.1

- 36 feet (10 973 mm) maximum parallel to joist or truss span.

    R603.1.1

- Two stories in height, 10 feet (3048 mm) maximum story height.

    R603.1.1

- 110 miles per hour (mph) maximum wind speed, Exposure A, B or C.

    R603.1.1

STEEL WALL FRAMING

- 70 psf (3.35 kN/m^2) maximum snow load.

R603.1.1

- Exterior wall shall be considered load bearing.

R603.1.1

- Offsets exceed 4 feet (1219 mm) in areas with wind speeds greater than 110 mph or in SDC D$_1$ or greater shall be considered separate braced wall line.

R603.1.2

- In-line framing shall have a maximum ¾-inch (19.1 mm) tolerance.

R603.1.2

B. Structural framing

- Tracks shall have a minimum flange width of 1⅜ inches (32 mm).

R603.2

- The maximum side-bend radius for load-bearing members shall be greater than $^3/_{32}$ inch (2.4 mm) or two times the uncoated steel thickness.

R603.2

1. Holes shall be:

    - A maximum 1½ inches wide and 4 inches (102 mm) in length.

R603.2

    - Along the centerline only.

R603.2

    - Not less than 24 inches (610 mm) center to center.

R603.2

    - Located no less than 10 inches (254 mm) from edge of hole to end of member unless patched.

R603.2

2. Materials

    - Load-bearing members shall be cold-formed and comply with ASTM standards.

R603.2.1

    - Load-bearing materials shall be identified by manufacturer, minimum uncoated thickness, minimum coating designation and minimum yield strength.

R603.2.1

- Load-bearing members shall have metallic coating per ASTM standards.

    R603.2.1

C. Fastening requirements

- Screws shall be self-drilling tapping with minimum ½-inch (12.7 mm) edge and center-to-center distances.

    R603.2.4

- Shall be minimum No. 8 for attaching sheathing to steel studs.

    R603.2.4

- Shall be minimum No. 6 for attaching gypsum board to studs.
    R603.2.4

- Shall verify minimum three exposed threads of penetration.
    R603.2.4

- The required number of screws is capable of being reduced.
    R603.2.4

D. Wall construction shall

- Comply with Section R603.3 and Figure R603.3.

    R603.3.1

- Be anchored to foundation or floors per Table R603.3.1 and Figure R603.3.1(1) or (2).

    R606.3.2

- Be fastened per Section R603.2.4 and Table R603.3.2(1).
    R606.3.2

- Have tracks the same thickness as studs.

    R606.3.2

- Be thinned when sheathing/wall coverings comply with Section R603.3.2.

    R606.3.2

- Stud bracing flanges will be laterally braced either per gypsum board with No. 6 screws or with horizontal steel strapping attached to studs. Straps shall be at least 1 ½ inches (38 mm) in width and 33 mils in thickness, attached with No. 8 screw.

    R603.3.3

STEEL WALL FRAMING

STEEL WALL FRAMING 55

- Straps shall be placed mid height on an 8-foot (2438 mm) wall and at one-third points for 9-foot and 10-foot (2743 mm and 3048 mm) walls.

R603.3.3

- Flanges and lips of studs and headers shall not be cut or notched.

R606.3.3

- Hole patching is required when stud web holes are closer than 10 inches (305 mm) to the end of member.

R603.3.5

- Steel studs and other structural members shall not be spliced.

R603.3.6

- The track shall be spliced per Figure R603.3.6.

R603.3.6

- Corners and top tracks shall comply with Figure R603.4.

R603.4

- The attachment of the exterior wall covering to steel stud walls shall be per manufacturer's requirements.

R603.5

E. Headers

- Headers shall be installed above wall openings in exterior walls per Tables R603.6(1), (2) and (3) and Section R603.6 or per AISI, *Standard for Header Design*.

R603.6

- King and jack studs shall be the same size as the adjacent wall studs and will comply with Table R603.6(4).

R603.6.1

- Headers of C-shape framing shall be connected per Table R603.6(5).

R603.6.1

- A clip-angle connection is required.

R603.6.1

- Half the total number of screws shall be applied to header, with a half total to king stud.

R603.6.1

F. Structural sheathing (wind speed less than 110 mph)

- A minimum of $^7/_{16}$-inch (11.1 mm) OSB or $^{15}/_{32}$-inch (11.9 mm) of plywood is required on all exterior wall surfaces.

    R603.7

- A minimum length of 20 percent of the braced wall length is required. The percentage shall include the full height, 48-inches (1120 mm) minimum width panels.

    R603.7

- The minimum percentage for full-height sheathing shall be multiplied by 1.10 for 9-foot (2743 mm) walls and 1.20 for 10-foot (3048 mm) walls.

    R603.7

- Sheathing shall be installed with long dimension parallel to studs.

    R603.7

- A minimum of a 48-inch-wide (1220 mm) panel for sheathing shall be applied to each corner of exterior walls.

    R603.7.1

- All edges and interior areas of structural panels shall be fastened to framing members.

    R603.7.1

- A single hold-down anchor is permitted to be installed at corners per Figure R603.1.3.

    R603.7.2

III. Wood Structural Panels

- Panels shall be identified by a grade mark or certificate of inspection.

    R604.1

- Maximum panel spans are not to exceed values from Table R602.3(3).

    R604.2

- Panels shall be attached to framing per Table R602.3(1).

    R604.3

- Wood panels marked "Exposure 1" or "Exterior" are considered water-repellent sheathing.

    R604.3

WOOD STRUCTURAL PANELS

MASONRY CONSTRUCTION

IV. Particleboard

- Particleboard shall be identified by a grade mark or certificate of inspection.

R605.1

- Particleboard grades shall comply with grades per Table R602.3(4).

R605.1

V. General Masonry Construction

- Masonry shall comply with ACI 530/ASCE 5/TMS 402 or Section R606.

R606.1

- A design professional is not required unless required by state law.

R606.1.1

A. Minimum thickness of masonry

- Masonry bearing walls that are more than one story high shall be 8 inches (203 mm).

R606.2.1

- Solid masonry for one-story buildings no more than 9 feet (2743 mm) in height, plus 6 feet (1829 mm) of gable permitted shall be 6 inches (152 mm).

R606.2.1

- A 16 inch (406 mm) minimum thickness is required for rough, random or crushed rubble stone.

R606.2.2

- A course of solid masonry is required between the wall below and the thinner wall above.

R606.2.3

- 8 inches (203 mm) minimum is required for unreinforced hollow unit masonry parapet walls; however, the height shall not exceed three times the thickness.

R606.2.4

- Solid masonry is required for corbelling:
  1. The maximum corbelling shall be half of the wall thickness or half the wythe for hollow walls.
  2. The maximum projection of one unit shall be one-half the height or one-third the thickness of the unit.

R606.3

57

- The top course of corbels shall be a header course when the masonry supports floor or roof members.

    R606.3
- Masonry may be supported on 8-inch (203 mm) foundation walls.

    R606.3.1
- Total horizontal projection shall not exceed 2 inches (51 mm); individual corbels shall be no more than one-third the thickness or half the height of the unit.

    R606.3.1
- Unsupported height of masonry piers shall not exceed 10 times their least dimension.

    R606.5
- Unfilled hollow piers shall be utilized when unsupported height is no more than four times the least dimension.

    R606.5
- 4 inches (102 mm) of solid masonry or concrete is required to cap hollow piers or have top course filled.

    R606.5.1
- Chases and recesses shall not be deeper than one-third wall thickness.

    R606.6
- The maximum length of the horizontal chase or projection shall not exceed a minimum of 4 feet (1219 mm) and shall have at least 8 inches (203 mm) of masonry in the back of the chase or recess.

    R606.6
- Masonry directly above chases or recesses wider than 12 inches (305 mm) shall be supported on noncombustible lintels.

    R606.1, .2, .3, .4 & .5
- Stack bond requires longitudinal reinforcement in horizontal bed joints no more than 16 inches (9406 mm) on center vertically.

    R606.7

MASONRY CONSTRUCTION

MASONRY CONSTRUCTION

- Verify lateral support per Table R606.8.
  1. Horizontal lateral support
  - 50-percent units overlaid, not less than 3 inches (76 mm) on unit below.
  - Metal reinforcement is required.

R606.8.1

  2. Vertical lateral support
  - Masonry walls shall be anchored to roof structures:
    - With metal straps per manufacturers' instructions.
    - With ½-inch (12.7 mm) approved anchor bolts, 6 feet (1829 mm) maximum on center.
  - Walls shall be anchored to floor diaphragm:
    - With metal straps per manufacturers' instructions.
    - With ½-inch (12.7 mm) bolts at a maximum of 6 feet (1829 mm) or with other approved methods.

R606.8.2

  - Masonry over openings shall be supported by:
    ○ Steel lintels.
    ○ Reinforced concrete.
    ○ Masonry or masonry anchors.

R606.9

  - Masonry walls shall be anchored to the floor and roof systems per Figure R606.10(1), (2) or (3).

R606.10

B. Seismic requirements
  1. Verify floor and roof diaphragms attachment:
  - Wood framing per Table R602.3(1).
  - Cold-formed steel floors per Table R505.3.1(2).
  - Cold-formed steel roofs per Table R804.3.
  - Blocking required at edges.
  - Fasteners SDC D_1 and D_2 shall be 4 inches (102 mm) on center.

R606.11.1.1

  2. Seismic Design Category C
  - Townhouses located in SDC C shall comply with this section.

a. Design elements not part of lateral force-resisting system.

- Masonry partition wall and masonry screen walls shall be reinforced per Figure R606.10(2).
R606.11.2.1.2
- Masonry elements shall be reinforced in either the horizontal or vertical direction.
R606.11.2.1.3

b. Design elements part of lateral-force-resisting system.

- Connections to masonry walls shall be provided.
R606.11.2.2.1
- Connections to masonry columns shall be provided.
R606.11.2.2.2
- Minimum reinforcement for masonry shear walls shall be installed.
R606.11.2.2.3

3. Seismic Design Category D_1

NOTE: All structures to comply with SDC C, plus this section.
R606.11.3

- Masonry structures limited to one story and 9 feet (2743 mm) between lateral supports need not be designed when complying with Sections R606.11.3.2 and 606.11.3.2.1.
R606.11.3.1
- Masonry elements per Section R606.11.2.1.2 or designed per Chapter 7, ACI.
R606.11.3.1
- Minimum reinforcement is required for masonry walls; vertical and horizontal required.
    - Maximum spacing shall be 48 inches (1219 mm) on center for solid grouted, hollow open units or two wythes of solid units.
    - Maximum spacing 24 inches (610 mm) for others.
R606.11.3.2
- Shear wall reinforcement required.
    - Spacing shall be the smaller of one-third length of the wall, one-third height of wall or 48 inches (1219 mm).

MASONRY CONSTRUCTION

MASONRY CONSTRUCTION

- Standard hook is required for anchoring around vertical rebars.
  R606.11.3.2.1
- Lateral ties for masonry columns spaced not more than 8 inches (203 mm) on center, at $^3/_8$ inch (9.5 mm) diameter, and shall be embedded in grout.
  R606.11.3.3
- Type N mortar or masonry cement is not required.
  R606.11.3.4
- Standard hooks shall be 135 degree or 180 degree.
  R606.11.3.5

4. Seismic Design Category D_2

NOTE: Structures shall comply with SDC D_1 requirements and Section R606.11.4.

a. Design elements not part of the lateral-force-resisting system:
  - Stack bond masonry reinforcement spacing is required and shall comply with Table R606.11.4.1.
    R606.4.1

b. Design elements part of the lateral-force-resisting system:
  - Stack bond masonry reinforcement is required and shall comply with Table R606.11.4.1.
    R606.4.2

c. Protection for rebar
  - All bars shall be completely embedded in mortar or grout.
    R606.12
  - $^5/_8$-inch (15.9 mm) mortar coverage is required for exposed force for joint reinforcement.
    R606.12
  - Other rebar minimum coverage of one bar diameter or ¾ inch (19.1 mm), whichever is greater.
    R606.12
  - Minimum coverage for rebar exposed to weather or soil shall be 2 inches (51 mm).
    R606.12

61

D. Beam supports

- Concentrated loads supported by wall or column shall have a minimum bearing of 3 inches (76 mm), metal bearing plate or a reinforced masonry member with a 4-inch (102 mm) projection from the wall.

R606.13

- Joists shall have a minimum bearing of 1½ inches (38 mm), supported per Figure R606.10(1).

R606.13

E. Metal accessories

- Minimum corrosion protection shall comply with Table R606.14.1.

R606.14

VI.　Unit Masonry

- Mortar shall be Type M or S.

R607.1.1

- Mortar shall be Type M, S or N for lateral-force-resisting systems in SDC A, B and C.

R607.1.2

- Mortar shall be Type M or S Portland cement lime or mortar cement for lateral-force-resisting systems in SDC D_1 and D_2.

R607.1.3

A. Placing mortar and masonry units

- Unless otherwise required on project drawings, head and bed joints $^3/_8$-inch (9.5 mm) thick.

R607.2.1

- Starter course shall not be less than ¼ inch (6.4 mm) and no more than ¾ inch (19.1 mm).

R607.2.1

1. Joint tolerances
   - Bed joint; $+^1/_8$ inch (3.2 mm)
   - Head joint: ¼ inch (6.4 mm), + $^3/_8$ inch (9.5 mm)
   - Collar joints: ¼ inch (6.4 mm), + $^3/_8$ inch (9.5 mm). See exceptions.

R607.2.1.1

B. Masonry unit placement

- Mortar shall extrude from joint to produce a tight joint.

R607.2.2

UNIT MASONRY

MULTIPLE WYTHE MASONRY

- Deep furrowing of bed joints that produces voids is not permitted; relaying ment is required whenever bond is broken after initial placement.

R607.2.2

- Surfaces shall be clean and free of deleterious materials.

R607.2.2

- Solid masonry units shall be laid with full head and bed joints.

R607.2.2.1

- All interior vertical joints designed to receive mortar shall be filled.

R607.2.2.1

- Hollow masonry units shall have all head and bed joints filled solid no less than thickness of face shell.

R607.2.2.2

C. Wall ties

- Ends shall be embedded in mortar joints.

R607.3

- Ties shall engage outer face shells by a minimum of ½ inch (12.7 mm).

R607.3

- Ends shall be embedded a minimum of 1½ inches (38 mm) into mortar bed of solid masonry units or solid grouted hollow units.

R607.3

- Ties shall not be bent after embedment.

R607.3

VII. Multiple Wythe Masonry

- Facing and backing shall be bonded per Section R608.1.1, 2 or 3.

R608.1

- Cavity walls shall have a minimum width of 3 inches (76 mm) for facing and backing; maximum cavity width of 4 inches (102 mm).

R608.1

- Backing shall be as thick as facing. See exceptions.

R608.1

A. Bonding with masonry headers
   1. Solid units
      - When masonry headers are used to bond, 4-percent minimum wall surface of each face shall have headers extending 3 inches (76 mm) minimum into backing.
        R608.1.1.1
      - Maximum distance between full-length headers shall not exceed 24 inches (610 mm) vertically or horizontally.
        R608.1.1.1
      - There shall be a minimum 3-inch (76 mm) overlap.
        R608.1.1.1
   2. Hollow units
      - Stretcher courses are required to be bonded at vertical intervals not exceeding 34 inches (864 mm) with 3-inch (76 mm) intervals.
        R608.1.1.2
      - Lapping at vertical intervals shall not exceed 17 inches (432 mm) with units minimum 50 percent greater in thickness than units below.
        R608.1.1.2
B. Bonding with wall ties or joint reinforcement
   1. Bonding with wall ties
      - There shall be one metal tie for each 4½ square feet (0.418 m^2).
        R608.1.2.1
      - A $^3/_{16}$-inch diameter (4.8 mm) wall tie shall be embedded in horizontal joints.
        R608.1.2.1
      - Ties shall be staggered in alternate courses.
        R608.1.2.1
      - There shall be a 24-inch (610 mm) maximum vertical distance between ties and a 36-inch (914 mm) maximum horizontal distance between ties.
        R608.1.2.1
      - Bent ties required.
        R608.1.2.1
      - Additional ties are required at openings and shall not be spaced more than 3 feet (914 mm) around the perimeter and within 12 inches (305 mm) of openings.

MULTIPLE WYTHE MASONRY

MULTIPLE WYTHE MASONRY

2. Bonding with adjustable wall ties
  - One tie is required for each 2.67 square feet (.25 m²) of wall area.
  R608.1.2.2
  - Spacing of ties shall not exceed 24 inches (610 mm) on center.
  R608.1.2.2
  - There shall be a 1¼-inch (32 mm) maximum vertical offset of bed joints.
  R608.1.2.2
  - A ¹/₁₆-inch (1.6 mm) maximum clearance is required between connecting parts of ties.
  R608.1.2.2
  - When used, two pintle legs ³/₁₆ inch in diameter (4.8 mm) are required.
  R608.1.2.2

3. Bonding with prefabricated joint reinforcement
  - One tie cross wire is required for each 2.67 square feet (.25 m²) of the wall area.
  R608.1.2.3
  - 16 inches (406 mm) maximum vertical spacing is required.
  R608.1.2.3
  - A minimum No. 9 gage is required.
  R608.1.2.3
  - Wires shall be embedded in the mortar.
  R608.1.2.3

C. Bonding with natural or cast stone

1. Ashlar masonry
  - Uniformly distributed bonder units shall be distributed to no less than 10 percent of the wall area.
  R608.1.3.1
  - Units shall not extend less than 4 inches (102 mm) into the wall.
  R608.1.3.1

2. Rubble stone masonry
  - Bonder units shall have a maximum horizontal spacing of 3-feet (914 mm).

- One bonder unit is required for each 6 square feet (.56 m^2) of wall space on both sides when masonry exceeds 24 inches (610 mm).

R608.1.3.2

D. Masonry bonding pattern

1. Running bond
   - Head joints shall be offset one-fourth of the unit length or masonry walls shall be reinforced per Section R608.2.2.

R608.2.1

2. Stack bond
   - Bond beams shall not be more than 48 inches (1219 mm) on center.

R608.2.1

VIII. Grouted Masonry

- Grout shall comply with ASTM C 476.

R609.1.1

- Maximum pour heights and minimum dimensions shall comply with Table R609.1.2.

R609.1.2

- The horizontal construction joint, 1 inch (25 mm) below top, is required when work is stopped 1 hour or longer.

R609.1.2

- Maximum mortar projections shall be ½ inch (12.7 mm) or removed.

R609.1.3

- Grout shall be placed before initial set, 1½ hours maximum after water is added.

R608.1.4

- Maximum lift is not to exceed 5 feet (1524 mm).

R609.1.4

- Aluminum pipes are not permitted for pumping grout.

R609.1.4.1

- As required by the building official, cleanouts shall be sealed after inspection and prior to grouting.

R609.1.5

- Multiple-wythe masonry requires cleanouts at bottom course when pour exceeds 5 feet (1524 mm) in height.

R609.1.5.1

GROUTED MASONRY

GROUTED MASONRY

- Hollow-unit masonry requires cleanouts at bottom course when pour exceeds 4 feet (1219 mm) in height.

R609.1.5.2

A. Grouted multiple-wythe masonry

- Grouted multiple-wythe masonry shall comply with Sections R609.1 and R609.2.

R609.2

- Masonry headers shall not be permitted where all interior spaces are grouted.

R609.2.1

- Metal ties are required.

R609.2.1

- Fine grout is required for any interior vertical space that does not exceed 2 inches (51 mm) in thickness.

R609.2.2

- Coarse or fine grout is permitted for spaces exceeding 2 inches (51 mm).

R609.2.2

- Solid masonry is required for vertical grout barriers.

R609.2.3

- Maximum spacing of 25 feet (7620 mm) is required for grout barriers.

R609.2.3

- Grouting between barriers shall be completed in one day with no interruptions greater than 1 hour.

R609.2.3

B. Reinforced grouted multiple-wythe masonry

- Masonry shall comply with Sections R609.1, R609.2 and R609.3.

R609.3

- Grout or mortar thickness shall not be less than ¼ inch (6.4 mm).

R609.3.1

- Steel wire reinforcement is required in horizontal mortar joints no less than twice the wire diameter.

R609.3.1

- C. Reinforced hollow unit masonry
- Masonry shall comply with Sections R609.1 and R609.4.
  R609.4
- Shall maintain an unobstructed vertical continuity of cells to be filled.
  R609.4.1
- Units shall be lapped in successive vertical courses.
  R609.4.1
- Cells to be filled shall comply with Table R609.1.2.
  R609.4.1
- Vertical reinforcement shall be held in place at the top and bottom at intervals not exceeding 200 diameters of the reinforcement.
  R609.4.1
- All reinforced cells shall be filled with grout.
  R609.4.1
- Lifts shall be a maximum of 8 feet (2438 mm).
  R609.4.1
- Grout poured over 8 feet (2438 mm) shall be placed in lifts not to exceed 5 feet (1524 mm); special inspection is required.
  R609.4.1
- Horizontal steel is required to be fully embedded by the grout.
  R609.4.1

IX. Glass Unit Masonry

- Hollow glass units shall have a minimum average face thickness of $3/16$ inch (4.8 mm).
  R610.2
- Surface shall be treated.
  R610.2
- The use of reclaimed units is prohibited.
  R610.2
- A. Units
- Standard units shall be a minimum $3^7/_8$ inches (98 mm) in thickness.
  R610.3

GLASS UNIT MASONRY

- Hollow units shall be a minimum of $3^{1}/_{8}$ inches (79 mm) in thickness.

R610.3

- Solid units shall be a minimum of 3 inches (76 mm) in thickness.

R610.3

B. Isolated panels

1. Exterior standard-unit panels
   - The maximum area is 144 square feet (13.4 m^2) when the design wind pressure is 20 psf (958 Pa).

R610.4.1

   - The maximum area shall comply with Figure R610.4.1 when wind pressure is other than 20 psf (958 Pa).

R610.4.1

   - The maximum dimension between structural supports is 25 feet (7620 mm) in width or 20 feet (6096 mm) in height.

R610.4.1

2. Exterior thin-unit panels
   - The maximum area of individual panels shall be 85 square feet (7.9 m^2).

R610.4.2

   - Maximum dimension between structural supports shall be 15 feet (4572 mm) in width or 10 feet (3048 mm) in height.

R610.4.2

3. Interior panels
   - The maximum area of individual standard unit panels shall be 250 square feet (23 m^2).

R610.4.3

   - The maximum area thin-unit panels is 150 square feet (14 m^2).

R610.4.3

   - The maximum distance between structural supports is 25 feet (7620 mm) in width or 20 feet (6096 mm) in height.

R610.4.3

4. Curved panels
   - The width shall comply with Sections R610.4.1, .2 and .3.

R610.4.4

- Additional structural supports are required where inflection points occur in multicurved walls.

  R610.4.4

C. Panel support

- The maximum total deflection of structural members supporting glass masonry is 1/600.

  R610.5

- Lateral supports are required along top and sides of panels.

  R610.5.2

- Lateral supports are to resist a minimum 200 pounds per lineal foot or actual applied load—whichever is greater.

  R610.5.2

- Lateral support shall be provided by panel anchors, top and sides that are spaced a maximum of 16 inches (406 mm) on center.

  R610.5.2

- Channel-type restraints are required for single-unit panels. See exceptions.

  R610.5.2

  1. Panel anchor restraints

     - The maximum spacing shall be 16 inches (406 mm) on center in both jambs and across the head.
     - Two fasteners per panel anchor are required with a minimum embedment of 12 inches (305 mm).

       R610.5.2.1

D. Sills

- Sill areas shall be covered with a minimum coating of $1/8$ inch thick (3.2 mm) prior to bedding of units.

  R610.6

E. Expansion joints

- Expansion joints are required along the top and sides of all structural supports, and shall be a minimum of $3/8$ inch thick (9.5 mm).

  R610.7

- Expansion joints shall be free of debris and shall be filled with resilient material.

  R610.7

GLASS UNIT MASONRY

GLASS UNIT MASONRY

F. Mortar

- Mortar shall be Type S or N.

R610.8

- Mortar shall not be retempered.

R610.8

- Unused mortar shall be discarded 1½ hours after initial mixing.

R610.8

G. Reinforcement

- Horizontal joint reinforcement shall be placed a maximum of 16 inches (406 mm) on center.

R610.9

- Horizontal joint reinforcement shall extend the full length of the panel but shall not extend across expansion joints.

R610.9

- Longitudinal wires shall have a minimum lap of 6 inches (152 mm) at splices.

R610.9

- Joint reinforcement is required in bed joint immediately below and above openings in panel.

R610.9

- Reinforcement shall not be less than two parallel wires, size W1.7 or greater.

R610.9

H. Placement

- Glass units shall be placed so head and bed joints are filled solid.

R610.10

- Mortar shall not be furrowed.

R610.10

- The minimum joint thickness is ¼ inch (6.4 mm).

R610.10

- Vertical joints of radial panels are ⅛ inch (3.2 mm) minimum or ⅝ inch (15.9 mm) maximum.

R610.10

- Bed joint tolerances are 1/16 inch (1.6 mm) and plus ⅛ inch (3.2 mm).

R610.10

- Head joint tolerance is plus or minus $^1/_8$ inch (3.2 mm).

    R610.10

X. Insulating Concrete Form (ICF) Wall

- Seal of the design professional is not required by code if the design and construction comply with ACI 318 or Section R611.1.

    R611.1

A. Applicability limits

- Plan dimensions shall not exceed 60 feet (18 288 mm).

    R611.2

- Floor dimension shall not exceed 32 feet (9754 mm).

    R611.2

- Roof-clear span shall not exceed 40 feet (12 192 mm).

    R611.2

- The maximum height shall be two stories [10 feet (3048 mm)].

    R611.2

- Walls shall be limited to buildings with a 150 mph (209 km/h) wind speed, a 70 psf (3.35 kN/m^2) ground snow load, and SDC A, B and C.

    R611.2

B. Flat ICF

- Flat ICF wall systems shall comply with Figure R611.3 and be reinforced per Table R611.3 and Section R611.7.

    R611.3

C. Waffle grid

- The waffle grid wall system shall comply with Figure R611.4 with reinforcement per Table R611.4(1) and Section R611.7.

    R611.4

- Minimum core dimensions shall comply with Table R611.4(2).

    R611.4

D. Screen grid

- A screen-grid wall system shall comply with Figure R611.5 with reinforcement per Table R611.5.

    R611.5

ICF WALLS

- Minimum core dimensions shall comply with Table R611.4(2).

R611.5

E. Material

1. Concrete
- Ready-mixed concrete for ICF walls shall comply with Section R402.2.

R611.6.1
- The maximum slump shall be 6 inch (152 mm).

R611.6.1
- The maximum aggregate size shall be ⅞ inch (19.1 mm).

R611.6.1
- A minimum concrete compressive strength of 3,000 pounds per square inch (psi) (20 685 kPa) shall be used for SDC D$_1$ and D$_2$.

R611.6.1

2. Reinforcing steel
- Minimum Grade 40 steel is required in SDC A, B, C.

R611.6.2
- Minimum Grade 60 steel is required in SDC D$_1$ and D$_2$.

R611.6.2

3. Insulation materials
- Thermal barrier is required on building interior.

R611.6.3
- Surface burning characteristics shall comply with Section R314.1.1.

R611.6.3

F. Wall construction
- ICF walls shall comply with Figure R611.7(1) and Section R611.7.

R611.7

1. Reinforcement
- Vertical and horizontal reinforcement shall be placed in the middle one-third of wall.

R611.7.1
- Concrete coverage shall comply with ACI 318. See exception.

R611.7.1.1

G. Vertical steel

- Above-grade walls shall be reinforced per Section R611.3, R611.4 or R611.5 and R611.7.2.

    R611.7.1.2

- Reinforcement in the top story shall terminate with a bend or standard hook, with a minimum lap splice of 24 inches (610 mm) with top horizontal reinforcement.

    R611.7.1.2

  1. Townhouses
     - For SDC C a minimum of one No. 5 bar is required at 24 inches (610 mm) on center or one No. 4 bar at 16 inches (407 mm) on center is required.

       R611.7.1.2

     - For SDC D_1 and D_2 a minimum of one No. 5 bar at 18 inches (457 mm) on center or one No. 4 bar at 12 inches (305 mm) on center is required.

       R611.7.1.2

  2. Above-grade ICF wall
     - Wall shall be supported on concrete foundations reinforced per wall above or per Tables R404.(1) through R404.4(5), whichever is greater.

       R611.7.1.2

     - Vertical steel shall be continuous from bottom of foundation wall to roof.

       R611.7.1.2

     - Dowels are required when vertical steel is not continuous, and shall be embedded 40 d_b or No. 6 or larger rebar embedded 24 inches (610 mm) into foundation wall with a standard hook.

       R611.7.1.2

H. Horizontal steel

- A minimum 4-inch-thick (102 mm) wall shall have a minimum of one No. 4 bar at 32 inches (812 mm) on center and one No. 4 bar within 12 inches (305 mm) of the top of the wall.

    R611.7.1.3

- A minimum 5½-inch (140 mm) or greater wall shall have a minimum of one No. 4 bar at 48 inches (1219 mm) on center and one No. 4 bar within 12 inches (305 mm) of the top of the wall.

    R611.7.1.3

  1. Townhouses in SDC C

ICF WALLS

ICF WALLS

- The minimum horizontal reinforcement shall be one No. 5 bar at 24 inches (610 mm) on center or one No. 4 bar at 16 inches (407 mm) on center.

R611.7.1.3

- Each end of horizontal reinforcement shall terminate with a standard hook or lap slice.

R611.7.1.3

2. All buildings in SDC D_1 and D_2

- Minimum horizontal reinforcement shall be one No. 5 at 18 inches (457 mm) on center or one No. 4 at 12 inches (305 mm) on center.

R611.7.1.3

- Reinforcement shall be continuous around corners, with a minimum lap of 24 inches (610 mm).

R611.7.1.3

- Horizontal reinforcement shall be continuous around building corner with the use of corner bars or bend bars with a minimum lap splice of 24 inches (610 mm).

R611.7.1.3

- Each end of horizontal reinforcement shall terminate with a standard hook or lap slice.

R611.7.1.3

3. Lap splices

- Splices shall have a minimum lap of 40 bar diameters of the smaller bar.

R611.7.1.4

- The maximum distance between noncontact bars at a splice shall not exceed 8 bar diameters.

R611.7.1.4

- The standard hook shall have a 180-degree bend plus 4d_b extension, but no less than 2½ inches (64 mm) or 90-degree bend plus 12d_b extension.

R611.7.1.5

I. Wall openings

- Openings shall have an 8 inch (203 mm) minimum depth of concrete for flat and waffle-grid ICF walls.

R611.7.2

- Openings shall have a 12 inch (305 mm) minimum depth of concrete for screen grid.

R611.7.2

- Verify Table R611.7(1) and Figure R611.7(2) for openings.
R611.7.2

- Reinforcement placed horizontally above or below opening shall extend a minimum of 24 inches (610 mm), in addition to requirements of Sections R611.3, .4, .5 and R611.7.1.
R611.7.2

- A 2-inch by 4-inch (51 mm by 102 mm) plate is required at the perimeter of all wall openings:
    - ½-inch (12.7 mm) anchor bolts shall be spaced a maximum of 24 inches (610 mm) on center.
    - Bolts shall be embedded a minimum of 4 inches (102 mm).
    - Minimum 1½-inch (38 mm) concrete is to cover the face of the wall. See exception.
R611.7.2

J. Lintels

- Lintels are required for all openings greater than or equal to 2 feet (610 mm) for flat or waffle-grid ICF walls.
R611.7.3

- Verify Figure R611.7(3) and Table R611.7(2) or (3) for flat walls.
R611.7.3

- Verify Figure R611.7(4) or R611.7(5) and Table R611.7(4) or R611.7(5) for waffle grid.
R611.7.3

- Verify Figure R611.7(6) or R611.7(7) for screen grid.
R611.7.3

- Figure R611.7(3) is required to be used for waffle-grid and screen-grid walls.
R611.7.3

- Lintel depth is required to be increased by height of wall directly above opening when lintel spans the entire length of the opening.
R611.7.3.1

K. Stirrups

- Flat walls should use a minimum No. 3 stirrup with maximum spacing of d/2.
R611.7.3.2

ICF WALLS

ICF WALLS 77

- Waffle-grid walls shall be a minimum two No. 3 stirrups in each vertical core.

R611.7.3.2

- Screen grid walls shall use one No. 3 stirrup. See exception.

R611.7.3.2

L. Horizontal reinforcement

- One No. 4 rebar shall be placed in top of the lintel.

R611.7.3.3

- Horizontal rebar shall be within 12 inches (305 mm) of the top or bottom reinforcement, with specific limitations and requirements.

R611.7.3.3

1. Load-bearing walls

- Verify Tables R611.7(2), (3), (8) for lintels in flat ICF load-bearing walls.

R611.7.3.4

- Verify Tables R611.7(4), (5) or (8) for lintels in waffle-grid ICF load-bearing walls.

R611.7.3.4

- Verify Table R611.7(6) or (7) for screen-grid ICF load-bearing walls.

R611.7.3.4

- Verify Table R611.7(9) for spans larger than those permitted by other tables.

R611.7.3.4

2. Nonload-bearing walls

- Verify Table R611.7(10) for lintels in all nonbearing ICF walls; stirrups are not required.

R611.7.3.5

M. Minimum length of wall without openings

- Wind velocity pressures from Table R611.7.4 shall be used to determine the amount of solid wall.

R611.7.4

- Townhouses in SDC C and all buildings in SDC D_1 and D_2 shall use Table R611.7(11) for the minimum amount of solid wall length; the greater amount required by seismic or wind shall apply.

R611.7.4

- Solid wall segments shall be a minimum of 24 inches (610 mm) in length for minimum percentage.

    R611.7.4

- The maximum distance between wall segments shall not exceed 18 feet (5486 mm).

    R611.7.4

- For a 24-inch (610 mm) solid wall segment, the full height of each story is required at all exterior wall corners.

    R611.7.4

- Wall openings in SDC D_1 and D_2 shall be 48 inches (1220 mm) minimum in length.

    R611.7.4

- Minimum nominal wall thickness shall be 5½ inches (140 mm) for all wall types.

    R611.7.4

N. ICF wall-to-floor connections

  1. Top bearing

     - Floors bearing on top of ICF foundation walls shall comply with Figure R611.8(1).

        R611.8.1

     - Wood sill plate anchors shall be ½ inch (12.7 mm) embedded a minimum of 7 inches (178 mm), with a maximum spacing no more than 6 feet (1829 mm) on center and 12 inches (305 mm) from corners.

        R611.8.1

     - Anchor bolts for waffle grid and screen grid shall be located in the core.

        R611.8.1

     - The maximum spacing of anchor bolts shall be 4 feet (1219 mm) where wind exceeds 90 mph.

        R611.8.1

     - Anchor bolts shall extend a minimum of 7 inches (178 mm) into concrete.

        R611.8.1

     - Sill plates require protection against decay.

        R611.8.1

     - Cold-formed steel framing shall be anchored per Section R505.3.1 or R603.3.1.

        R611.8.1

  2. Ledger bearing requirements for SDC C, D_1 and D_2

ICF WALLS

- Additional anchorage shall be used for townhouses in SDC C and all buildings in SDC D_1 and D_2.

R611.8.2.1

- Additional anchorage shall be installed through an oversized, ½-inch (12.7 mm) hole in the ledger board.

R611.8.2.1

- Blocking shall be attached to the floor or roof sheathing.

R611.8.2.1

- Toe nails or nails subject to withdrawal shall not be used.

R611.8.2.1

- Threaded rods with hex nuts shall comply with ASTM A 307 or ASTM F 1554.

R611.8.2.1

- Anchor bolts shall be embedded per Table R611.9; however, bolts with hooks are not required.

R611.8.2.1

- Floor and roof diaphragms shall comply with Table R602.3(10) or R602.3(2); cold-formed steel roof framing shall comply with Table R804.3.

R611.8.3

- Edge spacing of fasteners in floor and roof sheathing for SDC D_1 and D_2 shall be:
  1. 4 inches (102 mm) on center for SDC D_1.
  2. 3 inches (76 mm) on center for SDC D_2.
  3. A minimum penetration by a fastener of $1^3/_8$ inches (35 mm) into framing members; wood structural panel shall be a minimum of $^7/_{16}$ inch (11 mm).

R611.8.3.1

O. Floor and roof diaphragm construction

- Wood sheathing panels shall be attached to wood framing per Table R602.3(1).

R611.8.3

- Cold-formed steel floor framing shall comply with Table R505.3.1(2) or R804.3.

R611.8.3

- Panel edges shall be blocked and edge fasteners spaced.

R611.8.3

79

- In SDC C, fasteners shall be 4 inches (102 mm) on center where the width-to-thickness ratio exceeds 2:1.

    R611.8.3

P. ICF wall to top sill plate (roof) connections

- A ½-inch (12.7 mm) anchor bolt shall be embedded a minimum 7 inches (178 mm) and spaced 6 feet (1829 mm) on center per Figure R611.9.

    R611.9

- Anchored bolts shall be located in cores of waffle-grid and screen-grid ICF walls.

    R611.9

- Rafter or truss ties are required per Table R802.11 where wind uplift pressure is 20 psf (958 Pa) or greater.

    R611.9

  1. SDC C, D_1 and D_2 requirements.

     NOTE: These requirements are in addition to Section R611.9 for ICF wall to top sill plate (roof) connection.

     - Gable end shall comply with Section R611.8.1.1.

        R611.9.1

     - Townhouses in SDC C shall have attic floor diaphragms of structural wood panels per Table R602.3(1) or R602.3(2).

        R611.9.1

     - In SDC D_1, attic floor sheathing shall be fastened 4 inches (102 mm) on center.

        R611.9.1

     - In SDC D_2, attic floor sheathing shall be fastened 3 inches (76 mm) on center.

        R611.9.1.

     - In SDC D_1 and D_2, all sheathing edges are blocked.

        R611.9.1

     - The minimum panel thickness shall be $7/16$ inch (11 mm) for attic floors.

        R611.9.1

     - Structural attic floors are not required for hipped roof construction.

        R611.9.1

ICF WALLS

WINDOWS AND DOORS

- Townhouses in SDC C shall have wood sill plates attached with Grade A 307 with $^3/_8$-inch (9.5 mm) bolts, embedded a minimum 7 inches (178 mm) with a maximum spacing of 36 inches (914 mm) on center.
R611.9.1
- All buildings in SDC D_1 shall have bolts 24 inches (610 mm) on center.
R611.9.1
- All buildings in SDC D_2 shall have bolts 16 inches (406 mm) on center.
R611.9.1
- Townhouses in SDC C shall have an 18-gauge angle bracket on each floor joist, with three 8d common nails per leg.
R611.9.1
- All buildings in SDC D_1 shall have an 18-gauge angle bracket on each floor joist, with four 8d common nails per leg.
R611.9.1
- All buildings in SDC D_2 shall have an 18-gauge angle bracket on each floor joist, with six 8d common nails per leg.
R611.9.1

2. Hipped roof construction—no attic floor
- In SDC C, each rafter shall be attached to the sill plate with an 18-gauge bracket, with three 8d common nails per leg.
R611.9.1
- All buildings in SDC D_1 shall have each rafter attached to the sill plate with an 18-gauge bracket and four 8d common nails per leg.
R611.9.1
- All buildings in SDC D_2 shall have each rafter attached to the sill plate with an 18-gauge bracket and six 8d common nails per leg.
R611.9.1

XI. Exterior Windows and Glass Doors

A. Wind-borne debris protection
- Protection from wind-borne debris shall comply with Section R301.2.1.2.
R613.4

B. Anchorage methods

- Anchorage shall be per manufacturer or provide equal or greater anchoring based on accepted engineering practice.

R613.5

1. Anchorage details
    - Products shall be anchored per Figures R613.5(1), (2), (3), (4), (5), (6), (7) and (8).

    R613.5.2

2. Masonry, concrete or other structural substrate
    - Where the wood shim or buck is less than 1½ inches thick (38 mm), windows and glass doors shall be anchored through the jamb, with the jamb clipped directly into the concrete or other substrate.

    R613.5.2.1

    - Where the wood shim or buck is greater than 1½ inches (38 mm), the buck shall be securely fastened.

    R613.5.2.1

    - Anchors shall be embedded into secured wood buck.

    R613.5.2.1

3. Wood or other approved framing material
    - Windows and glass doors shall be anchored through the frame, by frame clip or anchored through the flange.

    R613.5.2.2

    - Anchors shall be embedded per Figures R613.5(6), (7) and (8).

    R613.5.2.2

C. Mullions occurring between individual window and glass door assemblies

- Mullions are to resist design pressure loads without deflecting more than L/175 (L = the span of mullions in inches).

R613.6

- Mullions require a structural safety factor one- and one-half times the design.

R613.6

WINDOWS AND DOORS

INTERIOR WALL COVERINGS

WALL COVERING

- Products are to be protected against adverse weather; there shall be no installation until weather protection is provided.
R701.2

- Exterior sheathing shall be dry before applying exterior cover.
R701.2

I. Interior Covering

- Interior coverings shall be installed per Tables R702.1(1), (2), (3) and Section 702.3.5.
R702.1

- Flame spread and smoke density shall comply with Section R315.
R702.1

- Interior masonry veneer shall comply with Sections R703.7.1 and R703.7.4—air space is not required.
R702.1

A. Interior plaster

- Plaster shall not be less than three coats when applied over metal lath and not less than two coats over other approved bases.
R702.2

- Veneer plaster may be applied in one coat and shall not exceed $^3/_{16}$ inch (4.76 mm) thickness.
R702.2

- Support spacing shall not exceed 16 inches (406 mm) for $^3/_8$ inch (9.5 mm) thick, or 24 inches (610 mm) for ½ inch (12.7 mm) thick.
R702.2.1

- Gypsum lath is required to be installed at right angles to support framing; end joints shall be staggered by one framing space.
R702.2.1

B. Gypsum board

- Wood framing shall have a minimum 2 inches (51 mm) of thickness. See exceptions.
R702.3.2

- Steel framing shall not be less than $1^1/_4$ inches (32 mm) wide.

  R702.3.3
  1. ICF walls
     - Foam plastic shall comply with Sections R404.4 and R611.

       R701.3.4
     - Interior habitable spaces are required to be covered per Section R318.1.2.

       R702.3.4
     - Adhesives may be used with mechanical fasteners and are required to be compatible with ICF materials.

       R702.3.4
  2. Application
     - The maximum spacing of supports and the size and spacing of fasteners shall comply with Table R702.3.5.

       R702.3.5
     - Gypsum sheathing shall be attached to exterior walls per Table R602.3(1).

       R702.3.5
     - Ends and edges of gypsum board shall occur on framing members, except on edges and ends perpendicular to the framing member.

       R702.3.5
     - Interior gypsum board shall not be installed when it is exposed to weather or to water.

       R702.3.5
  3. Fastening
     - Type W or Type S screws shall be used with a minimum $^5/_8$-inch (15.9 mm) penetration into wood.

       R702.3.6
     - Type S screws shall be used with a minimum $^3/_8$-inch (9.5 mm) penetration into steel.

       R702.3.6

C. Ceramic tile
  1. Gypsum backer
     - Water-resistant gypsum backing board is permitted on ceilings:
       - 16 inches (406 mm) maximum on center for $^5/_8$-inch (15.9 mm) gypsum board.

INTERIOR WALL COVERINGS

INTERIOR WALL COVERINGS

- o 12 inches (305 mm) maximum on center for ½-inch (12.7 mm) gypsum board.

R702.4.2

- All cut or exposed edges shall be sealed per manufacturer; this includes wall intersections.

R702.4.2

- Water-resistant gypsum board shall not be installed in shower or tub compartments over vapor retarder.

R702.4.2

- Limitations for water-resistant gypsum backing board:
  - o Over vapor retarder in shower or bathtub compartment.
  - o Where there is direct exposure to water or in areas subject to continuous high humidity.

R702.4.3

D. Other finishes

- Framing supports for wood veneer and hardboard paneling shall have a maximum spacing of 16 inches (406 mm) on center.

R702.5

- Wood veneer and hardboard paneling less than ¼ inch (6.4 mm) is required to have a ³/₈-inch (9.5 mm) gypsum board backer.

R702.5

E. Wood shakes and shingles

- Shakes and shingles shall be installed directly on studs with a minimum spacing of 24 inches (610 mm) on center.

R702.6

- Two nails or staples are required for each shake or shingle.

R702.6.1

- Fasteners are required to be covered by course above.

R702.6.1

1. Furring strips

- Strips shall be spaced 1 inch by 2 inches (25 mm by 51 mm) or 1 inch by 3 inches (25 mm by 76 mm) equal to exposure.

R702.6.2

- Furring strips are required to be nailed through wall material into studs.

R702.6.2

II. Exterior Covering

- Exterior walls shall provide weather-resistant exterior wall envelope.

  R703.1

- Exterior wall is to be designed and constructed to prevent accumulation of water within wall assembly.

  R703.1

- Water-resistive barrier behind exterior veneer shall comply with Section R703.2.

  R703.1

A. Weather-resistant sheathing paper

- When required by Table R703.4, asphalt-saturated felt or other approved material shall be applied over studs or sheathing.

  R703.2

- Material is required to be applied horizontally, with the upper layer lapped 2 inches (51 mm) over the lower layer.

  R703.2

- Vertical joints shall be lapped no less than 6 inches (152 mm). See exceptions.

B. Wood, hardboard and wood structural panel siding

  1. Panel siding

     a. Vertical joints

        - Shall occur over framing members unless wood or wood structural panel sheathing is used.
        - Shall be shiplapped or covered with batten.

          R703.3.1

     b. Horizontal joints

        - 1-inch (25 mm) minimum lap, shipped or flashed.
        - Shall occur over solid blocking, wood or wood structural panel sheathing.

          R703.3.3.1

  2. Horizontal siding

     - Siding shall be lapped a minimum of 1 inch (25 mm) or ½ inch (12.7 mm) if rabbeted.

       R703.3.2

EXTERIOR WALL COVERINGS

EXTERIOR WALL COVERINGS

- Ends shall be caulked, covered with batten or sealed and installed over flashing strip.

R703.3.2

C. Attachments

- All wall coverings shall be securely fastened per Table R703.4, or with other approved corrosion-resistant fasteners.

R703.4

D. Wood shakes and shingles

1. Application

   - Shall be applied over ½-inch (12.7 mm) wood-base sheathing, or furring strips over ½-inch (12.7 mm) nonwood sheathing.

   R703.5.1

   - A weather-resistant permeable membrane is required over all sheathing.

   R703.5.1

   - Horizontal overlaps shall not be less than 2 inches (51 mm), and vertical overlaps shall not be less than 6 inches (152 mm).

   R703.5.1

   - Furring strips shall be 1 inch by 3 inches or 1 inch by 4 inches (25.4 mm by 76 mm or 25.4 mm by 102 mm).

   R703.5.1

   - Furring strips are required to be fastened horizontally to studs with 7d or 8d box nails.

   R703.5.1

   - Furring strips are required to be spaced a distance on center equal to actual weather exposure, and shall not exceed Table R703.5.2.

   R703.5.1

   - Spacing between adjacent shingles shall not exceed ¼ inch (6.4 mm); spacing between adjacent shakes shall not exceed ½ inch (12.7 mm).

   R703.5.1

   - Spacing between joints in adjacent courses shall be a minimum of 1½ inches (38 mm).

   R703.5.1

   - Weather exposure shall not exceed requirements of Table R703.5.2.

   R703.5.2

2. Attachment
   - Each shake or shingle shall be fastened with two hot-dipped, zinc-coated, stainless steel or aluminum nails or staples.
     R703.5.3
   - Penetration of fasteners into sheathing shall be ½ inch (12.7 mm) minimum and shall not be overdriven.
     R703.5.3

   a. Staple attachment
      - Staple shall be no less than 16 gage and the crown width shall be no less than $7/16$ inch (11.1 mm).
        R703.5.3.1
      - The crown shall be parallel with the butt of the shake or shingle.
        R703.5.3.1

   b. Single-course application
      - Fasteners shall be concealed by course above.
        R703.5.3.1
      - Fasteners shall be driven approximately 1 inch (25 mm) above butt line and ¾ inch (19.1 mm) from edge.
        R703.5.3.1

   c. Double-course application
      - Exposed shake or shingle shall be face-nailed with two casing nails, driven approximately 2 inches (51 mm) above butt line and ¾ inch (19.1 mm) from each edge.
        R703.5.3.1

   d. All applications
      - Staples shall be concealed by course above.
        R703.5.3.1
      - Two additional nails are required with shingles wider than 8 inches (203 mm), and shall be 1 inch (25 mm) apart near center of shingle.
        R703.5.3
      - Bottom courses shall be doubled.
        R703.5.4

EXTERIOR WALL COVERINGS

EXTERIOR PLASTER

E. Exterior plaster

1. Lath
   - Shall be of corrosion-resistant materials.
   R703.6.1
   - Shall be attached with 1½-inch-long (38 mm) 11 gage nails, having a 7/16-inch (11.1 mm) head, or 7/8-inch-long (22.2 mm), 16 gage staples spaced 6 inches (152 mm) apart.
   R703.6.1

2. Plaster
   - There shall be no less than three coats of Portland cement plaster over metal lath or wire lath.
   R703.6.2
   - There shall be no less than two coats over masonry, concrete or gypsum backing.
   R703.6.2
   - Two coats are permitted when plaster surface is completely concealed.
   R703.6.2
   - Exterior plaster is to cover, but not extend below, lath, paper and screen on wood-frame construction.
   R703.6.2

3. Weep screeds
   - Shall be minimum No. 26 galvanized sheet gage corrosion resistant or plastic.
   R703.6.2.1
   - Shall have a minimum vertical attachment flange of 3½ inches (89 mm).
   R703.6.2.1
   - Shall be a minimum of 4 inches (102 mm) above earth or 2 inches (51 mm) above paved areas.
   R703.6.2.1
   - Shall be of type to allow trapped water to drain to exterior of building.
   R703.6.2.1
   - The weather-resistant barrier shall lap the attachment flange.
   R703.6.2.1
   - Exterior lath shall cover and terminate on the attachment flange of weep screed.
   R703.6.2.1

F. Stone and masonry veneer, general

- Shall be installed per Chapter 7, Table R703.4 and Figure R703.7.

  R703.7

- Veneer is limited to the first story above grade.

  R703.7

- There shall be a 5-inch (127 mm) maximum thickness when installed over backing of wood or cold-formed steel. See exceptions.
  1. Interior veneer support
     - Wood or cold-formed steel floors are required as support for interior veneer wall finishes.

       R703.7.1
  2. Exterior veneer support

     (Required, except in SDC D_1 and D_2)

     - Wood or cold-formed steel is required as supports for exterior masonry veneers, 40 psf (1915 Pa) or less.

       R703.7.2
     - Movement joint is required between foundation supported veneer and wood or cold-formed steel supported veneer.

       R703.7.2
     - Deflection is limited to 1/600 of span.

       R703.7.2

     a. Support by steel angle
        - A minimum 6-inch by 4-inch by $^5/_{16}$-inch (152 mm by 102 mm by 8 mm) steel angle, with a long leg vertical shall be anchored to double 2-inch by 4-inch (51 mm by 102 mm) wood studs, 16 inches (406 mm) on center, with a minimum of two $^7/_{16}$-inch (11.1 mm) diameter by 4-inch (102 mm) lag screws.

          R703.7.2.1
        - A minimum two-thirds width of veneer shall bear on steel angle.

          R703.7.2.1
        - Flashing and weep holes shall comply with Figure R703.7.1.

          R703.7.2.1

EXTERIOR VENEER

EXTERIOR VENEER

- The maximum height above angle shall be 12 feet 8 inches (3861 mm).

R703.7.2.1

- The maximum slope of the roof without stops shall be 7:12. Roofs with slopes more than 7:12 shall have stops 3 inch by 3 inch by $^1/_4$ inch (76 mm by 76 mm) welded along angle or as approved by the building official.

R703.7.2.1

- Air space between masonry and wood backing shall comply with Section R703.7.4 and R703.7.4.2.

R703.7.2.1

b. Support by roof construction

- Steel angle is required to be placed directly on top of roof construction.

R703.7.2.2

- A minimum of three 2-inch by 6-inch (51 mm by 152 mm) wood members shall be used for steel-angle support.

R703.7.2.2

- Connection to vertical wall shall use a minimum of three $^5/_8$-inch (15.9 mm) by 5-inch (127 mm) lag screws to every stud.

R703.7.2.2

- Additional roof members shall be anchored with two 10d nails at every stud.

R703.7.2.2

- A two-thirds width of veneer is required to bear on steel angle with a 12 foot 8 inch (3861 mm) height.

R703.7.2.2

- Air space between masonry and wood backing shall comply with Sections R703.7.4 and R703.7.4.2.

R703.7.2.2

- Roofs 7:12 but no more than 12:12 shall have stops of a minimum 3-inch by 3-inch by $^1/_4$-inch (76 mm by 76 mm by 6 mm) steel plate welded 24 inches (610 mm) on center or as approved by building official.

R703.7.2.2

3. Lintels
    - Masonry veneer shall not support any vertical load other than the veneer above.
      R703.7.3
    - Noncombustible lintels shall be used for openings, with an allowable span per Table R703.7.1.
      R703.7.3
    - Shall have a minimum 4-inch (102 mm) bearing.
      R703.7.3
4. Anchorage
    - Corrosion-resistant metal ties are required.
      R703.7.4
    - The maximum clearance between veneer and sheathing material shall be 1 inch (25 mm) for corrugated sheet metal tie.
      R703.7.4
    - The maximum clearance between veneer and wood backing shall be 4½ inches (11.4 mm) for metal strand wire ties.
      R703.7.4
    - Adjustable metal strand wire ties are required where veneer is anchored to cold-formed steel; a 4½-inch (114 mm) maximum separation is required.
      R703.7.4

    a. Size and spacing
        - Strand wire shall not be less in thickness than No. 9 U.S. gage, spaced no more than 24 inches (610 mm) on center, supporting no more than 3¼ square feet (.3 m^2) of wall area.
          R703.7.4.1
        - Corrugated sheet metal shall not be less in thickness than No. 22 U.S. gage minimum by $^7/_8$ inch (22.3 mm), spaced not more than 24 inches (610 mm) on center and supporting no more than 2.67 square feet (.25 m^2) of wall area.
          R703.7.4.1

    b. Veneer ties around wall openings
        - Additional ties are required when wall openings exceed 16 inches (406 mm) in either dimension.
          R703.7.4.1.1

EXTERIOR VENEER

EXTERIOR VENEER

  o Metal ties shall be spaced no more than 3 feet (9144 mm) on center and within 12 inches (305 mm) of wall opening.
  R703.7.4.1.1

5. Air space
   - A minimum of 1 inch (25 mm), and a maximum of 4½ inches (114 mm) of air space is required between veneer and sheathing.
   R703.7.4.2
   - Weather-resistant membrane or asphalt-saturated felt is not required over water-repellent sheathing materials.
   R703.7.4.2

6. Mortar or grout fill
   - 1 inch (25 mm) of air space is required to be filled with grout.
   R703.7.4.3
   - Wire mesh and approved paper or paper-backed reinforcement is required as replacement sheathing for weather-resistant membrane or asphalt-saturated felt.
   R703.7.4.3

7. Flashing
   - Flashing is required beneath the first course of masonry above finished ground level.
   R703.7.5
   - See additional requirements per Section R703.8.
   R703.7.5

8. Weep holes
   - Holes are required in outside wythe of masonry walls.
   R703.7.6
   - Maximum spacing shall be 33 inches (838 mm) on center.
   R703.7.6
   - Holes shall be a minimum of $3/16$ inch (4.8 mm) in diameter.
   R703.7.6
   - Holes shall be located immediately above the flashing.
   R703.7.6

G. Flashing
   - Flashing shall be of an approved corrosion-resistant material.
   R703.8

- Flashing is required in exterior wall envelope and shall extend to surface of exterior wall finish.

    R703.8

- Flashing is installed to prevent water from reentering wall envelope at the following locations:

    1. Top of all exterior window and door openings except self-flashing windows; jamb flashing may be omitted when approved by the building official.
    2. Intersection of chimneys or masonry construction and frame or stucco walls.
    3. Under and at ends of masonry, wood or metal coping and sills.
    4. Above all projecting wood in a continuous fashion.
    5. Where porches, decks or stairs attach to the wall or floor assembly of wood-framed construction.
    6. Wall and roof intersections.
    7. Built-in gutters.

    R703.8

H. Exterior insulation finish systems (EIFS)

- Shall be installed per manufacturers' installation instructions.

    R703.9

- Decorative trim shall not be nailed through EIFS.

    R703.9

- EIFS shall terminate no less than 6 inches (152 mm) above the finished ground level.

    R703.9

- A weather-resistant barrier is required between the building components and exterior insulation.

    R703.9.1

- A weather-resistant barrier shall be applied horizontally, with a 2-inch (51 mm) minimum horizontal lap and 6-inch (152 mm) minimum vertical lap.

    R702.9.1

- Flashing per Section R703.8.

    R703.9.2

I. Fiber cement siding

   1. Panel siding

EXTERIOR VENEER

EXTERIOR VENEER

- Panels shall be installed with the long dimension parallel to framing.

R703.10.1

- Vertical joints shall occur over framing members.

R703.10.1

- Vertical joints shall be sealed or covered with battens.

R703.10.1

- Horizontal joints shall be flashed with Z-flashing and blocked with solid wood framing.

R703.10.1

2. Horizontal lap siding

- Shall be lapped a minimum of 1 1/4 inches (32 mm) with ends sealed with caulking and covered with H-section joint cover or located over strip of flashing.

R703.10.2

- Fastener heads shall be exposed or concealed, depending on manufacturers' installation instructions.

R703.10.2

ROOF-CEILING CONSTRUCTION

> NOTE: Roof and ceiling construction shall be capable of carrying all loads and transmitting them to structural elements.
>
> R801.2

I. Roof Drainage

- A controlled method of water disposal is required where expansive or collapsible soils exist.

    R801.3

- Roof drainage shall be collected and then discharged a minimum of 5 feet (1524 mm) away from the foundation walls, or with an approved drainage system.

    R801.3

II. Wood Roof Framing

- A grade mark or certificate of inspection is required for all load-bearing lumber.

    R802.1

- Approved end-jointed lumber may be used interchangeably with the same species and grade solid sawn lumber.

    R802.1

- A grade mark is required on all fire-retardant-treated lumber; the moisture content shall be 19 percent or less for lumber, and 15 percent or less for wood structural panels.

    R802.1.3.2

- Strength adjustments shall be required for fire-retardant-treated materials.

    R802.1.3.1

- Roof-ceiling assemblies shall be designed and constructed per Chapter 8 and Figures R606.10(1), (2) and (3) or per NFPA/NDS.

    R802.2

- Roof ceilings shall be fastened per Table R602.3(1).

    R802.2

A. Framing details

- Rafters shall be framed to ridge board or to each other with a gusset plate as a tie.

    R802.3

WOOD ROOF FRAMING

- Ridge board shall be a minimum of 1 inch (25 mm) thick, and the depth shall be no less than the cut end of rafters.
R802.3

- Minimum 2-inch (51 mm) valley or hip rafters, and the depth shall be no less than the cut end of rafters.
R802.3

- Hip and valley rafters shall be supported at the ridge or be designed.
R802.3

- Ridge beams, hips and valleys shall be designed as beams when the roof slope is less than 3:12.
R802.3

- Ceiling joists shall be continuous or securely joined at partitions.
R802.3.1

- Ceiling joists shall be nailed to adjacent rafters for continuous tie when the joists and rafters are parallel.
R802.3.1

- When joists and rafters are not parallel, subflooring or metal straps are required to provide a continuous tie, or 1-inch by 4-inch (25 mm by 102 mm) cross ties shall be used.
R802.3.1

- A designed girder is required where ceiling joists or rafter ties are not provided at top plate.
R802.3.1

- Rafter ties shall be spaced no more than 4 feet (1219 mm) on center.
R802.3.1

- A 3-inch (76 mm) minimum lap is required for ceiling joists or they shall be butted over bearing partition and toe nailed.
R802.3.2

- Ceiling joists used to resist rafter thrust shall be nailed per Table R602.3(1), and butted joists shall be tied together.
R802.3.2

B. Allowable ceiling joist spans

- Spans shall comply with Tables R802.4(1) and R802.4(2).
R802.4

97

C. Allowable rafter spans
- Spans shall comply with Tables R802.5.1(1) through R802.5.1(8).

    R802.5

- The span shall be measured along the horizontal projection of the rafter.

    R802.5

- Verify:
    1. Species and grade of lumber.
    2. Joist spacing.
    3. Live load and dead load.
    4. Size of rafter used—depth and width.
    5. Ceiling attached to rafters—cathedral ceiling.
    6. Ceilings not attached to rafters.

    R802.5

1. Purlins
    - Purlins are required to be at least the same size as rafters.

        R802.5.1

    - Purlins shall be installed per Figure R802.5.1.

        R802.5.1

    - Purlins shall be continuous and be supported by 2-inch by 4-inch (51 mm by 102 mm) braces.

        R802.5.1

    - Braces shall be installed no less than 45 degrees from horizontal.

        R802.5.1

    - Braces shall be spaced no more than 4 feet (1219 mm) on center.

        R802.5.1

    - The unbraced length of brace shall not exceed 8 feet (2438 mm).

        R802.5.1

D. Bearing
- Ends shall be a minimum of 1½ inches (38 mm) on wood or metal.

    R802.6

CUTTING AND NOTCHING

- Ends shall bear a minimum of 3 inches (76 mm) on masonry or concrete.

R802.6

- If there is finished ceiling material already installed, a compression strip shall be used.

R802.6.1

E. Cutting and notching

- Cutting, boring or notching shall comply with Section R802.7.

R802.7.1

1. Sawn lumber; notches

- Notch depth shall be no more than one-sixth the depth of the member.

R802.7.1

- Notch length shall be limited to a one-third member depth for length.

R802.7.1

- Notches shall not be located in middle one-third of span.

R802.7.1

- A one-fourth depth maximum is required for notches at the ends of the member.

R802.7.1

- The tension side of members 4 inches (102 mm) or greater shall not be notched except at ends.

R802.7.1

- A limitation of one-third member depth is required for holes, bored or cut.

R802.7.1

- Holes shall not be permitted within 2 inches (51 mm) of the top or bottom of the member, or any other hole.

R802.7.1

- Holes and notches shall not be permitted within 2 inches (51 mm) of each other.

R802.7.1

2. Engineered wood products

- There shall be no cuts, notches and holes in laminated veneer lumber, glue-laminated members or I-joists.

R802.7.2

F. Lateral support

- Rafters and ceiling joists exceeding 2 inches by 10 inches (51 mm by 254 mm) shall be laterally braced at bearing points.

    R802.8

- Rafters and ceiling joists over 2 inches by 12 inches (51 mm by 205 mm) shall be supported laterally by solid blocking, diagonal bridging (wood or metal) on continuous 1-inch by 3-inch (25 mm by 76 mm) wood strips nailed at intervals not exceeding 8 feet (2438 mm).

    R802.8

G. Framing of openings

- Header and trimmer joists are required.

    R802.9

- Single member for opening is permitted when header joist does not exceed 4 feet (1219 mm) maximum.

    R802.9

- Single trimmer may be used to carry a single header joist that is located within 3 feet (914 mm) of the trimmer joist bearing.

    R802.9

- Trimmers and headers shall be doubled when the opening exceeds 4 feet (1219 mm).

    R802.9

- Approved hangers are required when the opening exceeds 6 feet (1829 mm).

    R802.9

- Approved framing anchors or ledger strips are required for tail joists exceeding 12 feet (3658 mm).

    R802.9

H. Wood trusses

- Truss drawings shall be approved before installation.

    R802.10.1

- Truss drawings shall be delivered to the job site.

    R802.10.1

- Truss drawings shall include, as a minimum, 12 items of information.

    R802.10.1

FRAMING OF OPENINGS

WOOD TRUSSES

- Truss drawings are required to be prepared by a registered design professional.

R802.10.2

- Trusses are required to be braced.

R802.10.3

- Truss members shall not be cut, notched, drilled, spliced or otherwise altered without a registered design professional's approval.

R802.10.4

- Alteration resulting in additional load (HVAC, water heater, etc.) shall not be permitted without verification.

R802.10.4

1. Truss to wall connection
   - Approved connectors shall be used with an uplift capacity no less than 175 pounds (79 kg).

R802.10.5

- For uplift pressures of 20 psf (957 Pa) or greater, use Section 802.11.

R802.10.5

I. Roof tie-down
   - Additional requirements shall apply based on roof assembly being subject to wind uplift pressures of 20 psf (957 Pa) or greater.

R802.11.1

- Uplift pressures shall be determined using Tables R301.2(2) and R301.2(3).

R802.11.1

- A continuous load path is required from rafter or truss ties to foundation.

R802.11.1

- Uplift pressure shall be determined using an effective wind area of 100 square feet (9.3 m²) and Zone 1 in Table R301.2(2).

R802.11.1

III. Roof Sheathing

- Spans for lumber sheathing shall comply with Table R803.1.

    R803.1

- Spaced lumber for wood shakes or shingles shall comply with Sections R905.7 and R905.8.

    R803.1

- Spaced lumber is not allowed in SDC D_2.

    R803.1

A. Wood structural panel sheathing

- Panels shall be grade marked or have a certificate of inspection.

    R803.2.1

- Panel grades shall comply with Table R503.2.1.1(1).

    R803.2.1

- Exposure durability shall comply with location and grade.

    R804.2.1.1

- Fire-retardant-treated plywood shall be graded.

    R803.2.1.2

- Maximum spans for panels shall not exceed values in Table R503.2.1.1(1).

    R803.2.2

- Joints shall be staggered or nonstaggered per Table R602.3(1) or APA E30 for wood and Table R804.3 for steel roof framing.

    R803.2.3

- Comply with Table R602.3(1) for wood and Table R804.3 for steel.

    R803.2.3

IV. Steel Roof Framing

- Elements shall be straight and free of any defects that would affect the structural performance.

    R804.1

A. Applicability limits

- Buildings no greater than 60 feet (18 288 mm) long perpendicular to joist rafter or truss span.

    R804.1.1

ROOF SHEATHING

STEEL ROOF FRAMING

- Building no greater than 36 feet (10 973 mm) wide parallel to joist span or truss.

R804.1.1

- Not more than two stories in height, with each story 10 feet (3048 mm) high.

R804.1.1

- Roof slope shall not be less than 3:12 or greater than 12:12.

R804.1.1

- Maximum wind speed shall be 110 mph.

R804.1.1

- Wind Zones A, B and C.

R804.1.1

- Ground snow load is a maximum of 70 psf (3352 Pa).

R804.1.1

- In-line framing is required between load-bearing studs and roof framing, with a maximum tolerance of ³⁄₄ inch (19.1 mm) center line to center line.

R804.1.2

- Roof trusses shall comply with AISI truss design.

R804.1.3

B. Structural framing

- Framing shall comply with Figure R804.2(1), Tables R804.2(1) and R804.2(2).

R804.2

- Holes in roof framing shall not exceed 1.5 inches (38 mm) in width or 4 inches (102 mm) in length per Figure R804.2(3).

R804.2

- Holes shall be located along centerline of web only.

R804.2

- Holes shall not be located less than 24 inches (610 mm) center to center.

R804.2

- Holes shall be located no less than 10 inches (254 mm) from the edge of the hole to edge of support per Section R804.3.6.

R804.2

- Material shall be cold formed to shape.

R804.2.1

103

- Material shall have approved identification.

    R804.2.1

- Load-bearing steel framing shall have corrosion-protected metallic coating.

    R804.2.3

- Screws shall be self-drilling tapping, installed with a minimum edge distance and center-to-center spacing of ½ inch (12.7 mm).

    R804.2.4

- Approved screws shall be installed per Section R805.

    R804.2.4

- Screws shall extend through steel a minimum of three exposed threads.

    R804.2.4

- Screw reduction shall be used for screws larger than No. 8 per Table R804.2.4.

    R804.2.4

C. Roof construction

- Roof systems shall comply with Figure R804.3 and be fastened per Table R804.3.

    R804.3

- Ceiling joists shall not exceed limits per Table R804.3.1(1) or R804.3.1(2).

    R804.3.1

- The minimum bearing for ceiling joists is 1½ inches (38 mm) and shall be connected to rafters per Figure R804.3.1(1) and Table R804.3.1(3).

    R804.3.1

- When ceiling joists are continuous and framed across interior bearing supports, the supports shall be within 24 inches (610 mm) of midspan.

    R804.3.1

- Bearing stiffeners are required per Section R804.3.8 and Figure R804.3.8.

    R804.3.1

- Ceiling joists shall be designed per Section R505 when the attic is used as an occupied span.

    R804.3.1

STEEL ROOF FRAMING

STEEL ROOF FRAMING

1. Ceiling joist bracing

- Bottom flanges of steel are required to be laterally braced per Section R702.

R804.3.2

- Top flanges shall be laterally braced per Table R804.3.1(1) or R804.3.1(2).

R804.3.2

- Lateral bracing is required per Figure R804.3.

R804.3.2

- Blocking or bridging is required between joists, in-line with a stop bracing at a maximum spacing of 12 feet (3658 mm) perpendicular to joists.

R804.3.2

- The third-point bracing span values from Table R804.3.1(1) or (2) shall be used for certain installations.

R804.3.2

2. Allowable rafter spans

- Spans shall not exceed limits set in Table R804.3.3(1).

R804.3.3

- Wind speeds shall be converted to equivalent ground snow loads per Table R804.3.3(2).

R804.3.3

- Rafter span shall be selected based on higher of ground snow load or snow load converted from wind speed.

R804.3.3

- Rafter support braces shall have a maximum length of 8 feet (2438 mm), connected to ceiling joist and rafter.

R804.2.3

- Rafters shall be connected to parallel ceiling joists per Figures R804.3 and R804.3.1(1) and Table R804.3.1(3).

R804.2.3

- Rafters are required to be connected to ridge member with a 2-inch by 2-inch (51 mm by 51 mm) clip angle per Figure R804.3.3.1 and Table R804.3.3.1.

R804.2.3

- Ridge member shall be fabricated and installed per Figure R804.3.3.1.

R804.3.3

- Roof cantilevers shall not exceed 24 inches (610 mm) per Figure R804.3.

    R804.3.3.2

- Roof cantilevers shall be supported by a header per Section R603.6 or by floor framing per Section R505.3.7.

    R804.3.3.2

D. Rafter bottom flange bracing

- Bottom flanges shall be continuously braced.

    R804.3.4

- The maximum spacing shall be 8 feet (2438 mm) and measured parallel to rafters.

    R804.3.4

- Bracing shall be installed per Figure R804.3.

    R804.3.4

- Blocking or bracing is required between rafters in-line, with a maximum spacing of 12 feet (3658 mm).

    R804.3.4

- Ends of continuous bracing are required to be fastened to blocking with a minimum of two No. 8 screws.

    R804.3.4

- There shall be no cutting or notching of flanges and lips of load-bearing members.

    R804.3.5

- Holes in web shall comply with Section R804.2.

    R804.3.5

E. Hole patching

- Hole patching is required when holes are located closer than 10 inches (254 mm) from the edge of hole to edge of bearing surface.

    R804.3.6

- The patch shall comply with Figure R804.3.6.

    R804.3.6

- The patch shall be fastened to web using No. 8 screws spaced no greater than 1 inch (25 mm) center to center, with a minimum edge distance of ½ inch (12.7 mm).

    R804.3.6

STEEL ROOF FRAMING

STEEL ROOF FRAMING

F. Splicing

- There shall be no splicing of rafters and other structural members, except ceiling joists.
R804.3.7
- Ceiling joists spliced at interior bearing points shall comply with Figure R804.3.7(1).
R804.3.7
- Splicing of track shall comply with Figure R804.3.7(2).
R804.3.7

G. Bearing stiffener

- Stiffener shall be fabricated from C-section or track section.
R804.3.7
- Fasteners shall comply with Figure R804.3.8.
R804.3.7
- Stiffeners shall extend the full depth of web, installed on either side.
R804.3.8

H. Headers

- Headers are required to support roof-ceiling framing above wall openings.
R804.3.9
- Header spans in bearing walls shall comply with Table R603.6(1).
R804.3.9

I. Framing of openings

- Headers and trimmers are required for openings.
R804.3.10
- The header joist span shall not exceed 4 feet (1210 mm).
R804.3.10
- Header and trimmer joists shall be fabricated per Figures R804.3.10(1) and (2).
R804.3.10
- Headers shall be connected to trimmers with clip angles.
R804.3.10
- Clip angles are to be the same thickness as a floor joist.
R804.3.10

107

- J. Roof tie-down
- Rafter-to-bearing wall ties are required when wind uplift pressures are 20 psf (957 Pa) or greater.

V. Ceiling Finishes

- Ceilings shall be installed as for interior wall finishes per Section R702.

R805.1

VI. Roof Ventilation

- Cross ventilation is required; this includes cathedral ceilings.

R806.1

- Ventilation openings shall be protected against entrance of rain or snow.

R806.1

- Corrosion-resistant wire mesh shall be used with minimum $1/_8$-inch (3.2m mm) and maximum ¼-inch (6.75 mm) openings.

R806.1

- The total net ventilating area shall be 1 to 150 of area, 1 to 300 with approved placements of ventilators or 1 to 300 with vapor barrier on warm side of ceiling.

R806.2

- Insulation shall not block the free flow of air; a minimum 1 inch (25 mm) is required between insulation and roof sheathing.

R806.3

VII. Attic Access

- Access is required when the attic area exceeds 30 square feet (2.7 m^2) with a vertical height of 30 inches (762 mm) or greater.

R807.1

- A rough opening a size of 22 inches by 30 inches (559 mm by 762 mm) is required for access.

R807.1

- Access shall be located in a hallway or readily accessible location.

R807.1

INSULATION CLEARANCE

VIII. Insulation Clearance

- A minimum clearance of 3 inches (76 mm) is required from recessed lighting fixtures, fan motors and other heat-producing devices. See exception.

R808.1

ROOF COVERINGS AND ASSEMBLIES

I. Roof Classification

- Roofs shall be covered per Sections R904 and R905.

    R902.1

- Class A, B or C roofing is required to be installed in areas designed by law requiring their use, or when roof is less than 3 feet (914 mm) from the property line.

    R902.1

- Roofs of brick, masonry, slate, clay or concrete roof tile, exposed concrete roof deck, ferrous or copper shingles or sheets and metal sheets or shingles shall be considered Class A roof covering.

    R902.1

- Each bundle of fire-retardant-treated shingles and shakes shall be marked for identification.

    R902.2

II. Weather Protection

- Roofs shall protect the interior of a building.

    R903.2

- Flashing is required to prevent moisture from entering the wall, roof and at intersections or penetrations through the roof plane.

    R903.1

- Metal flashing shall be minimum No. 26 galvanized gage and corrosion resistant.

- Flashing is required at:

    1. Wall and roof intersections.

    2. Changes in roof slope or direction.

    3. Around roof openings.

    R903.2

A. Coping

- Noncombustible, weatherproof materials with a minimum width equal to the thickness of the parapet are required for capping at the parapet.

    R903.3

ROOF DRAINAGE

B. Roof drainage

- Roof drains are required unless the roof is sloped to drain over edges.

R903.4

- Roof drains are required at each low point.

R903.4

- Scuppers shall be placed level with the roof in the wall or parapet.

R903.4

- Overflow drains shall be the same size as roof drains.

R903.4.1

- Scuppers shall be a minimum three times the size of roof drains, a minimum of 4 inches (102 mm) in height and 2 inches (51 mm) above low point; overflow drains shall not be connected to roof drain lines.

R903.4.1

III. Materials

- Roof assemblies shall be compatible to each other and with the building or structure.

R904.2

- Approved materials are required.

R904.3

- Materials shall be delivered in packages with the manufacturers' identifying marks.

R904.4

IV. Roof Covering Requirements

A. Asphalt shingle

- A solid sheathed deck is required.

R905.2.1

- Shingles limited to use on roofs with slopes of 2:12 or greater.

R905.2.2

- With a 2:12 to 4:12 roof slope, double underlayment is required.

R905.2.2

- Fasteners shall be galvanized steel, stainless steel, aluminum or copper nails, minimum 12 gage with a $^3/_8$-inch (9.5 mm) head.

    R905.2.5

- Fasteners to penetrate into roofing a minimum of ¾ inch (19.1 mm).

    R905.2.5

- When the roof sheathing is less than ¾ inch (19.1 mm), fasteners shall penetrate through the sheathing.

    R905.2.5

- Fasteners shall comply with manufacturers' general requirements:
    - Four fasteners per strip shingle.
    - Two per individual shingle.

    R905.2.6

- Special methods are required when the:
    - Roof slope is greater than 20:12.
    - Basic wind speed exceeds 110 mph.

    R905.2.6

1. Underlayment
    - Underlayment shall be minimum two layers for roofs with slopes of 2:12 to 4:12.

        R905.2.7

    - Underlayments shall be minimum one layer for slopes over 4:12.

        R905.2.7

    - Horizontal laps shall be minimum 2 inches (51 mm).

        R905.2.7

    - End laps shall be offset a minimum of 6 feet (1829 mm).

        R905.2.7

2. Ice protection
    - Protection is required in areas where the average daily temperature is 25°F (-4°C) or less, or where required by the building official.

        R905.2.7.1

    - Two layers of underlayment are required.

        R905.2.7.1

ASPHALT SHINGLES

ASPHALT SHINGLES

- Underlayment shall extend minimum of 24 inches (610 mm) inside the exterior wall.

R905.2.7.1

- Special provisions shall apply to underlayment in high-wind areas. See exceptions.

R905.2.7.2

3. Flashing

- Base and cap flashing shall be installed per manufacturers' instructions.

R905.2.8.1

- Base flashing shall be either corrosion-resistant metal or mineral surface roll roofing.

R905.2.8.1

4. Valleys

- Three types are required:
  o For open valley (valley lining exposed), valley lining shall be a minimum of 24 inches (610 mm) wide and comply with Table R905.2.8.2.
  o For open valley, valley lining shall be two plies of mineral-surface roofing.
  o For closed valley, valley shall be covered with shingles.

R905.2.8.2

5. Crickets and saddles

- A cricket or saddle is required on the ridge side of chimneys greater than 30 inches (762 mm) wide.

R905.2.8.3

- Step flashing is required at the vertical sidewall.

R905.2.8.4

- For flashing against the vertical front wall, soil stack, vent pipe or chimney, flashing is applied per asphalt shingle manufacturers' instructions.

R905.2.8.5

B. Clay and concrete tile

- Tile may be installed over solid sheathing or spaced structural sheathing boards.

R905.3.1

- Tile shall be installed on roof slopes of 2½:12 or greater.

R905.3.2

113

- Double underlayment is required for roof slopes of 2½:12 to 4:12.

    R905.3.3.1

- Minimum one layer of underlayment is required for roof slopes of 4:12 or greater.

    R905.3.3

- Special provisions apply for underlayment in high-wind zones.

    R905.3.3.3

- The strength of concrete roof tile shall comply with ASTM C 1492.

    R905.3.5

- Corrosion-resistant fasteners with a ¾-inch (19.1 mm) penetration or through thickness of deck are required.

    R905.3.6

- Perimeter fastening shall include three tile courses no less than 36 inches (914 mm) from either side of hips or ridges and edges of eaves and gable rakes.

    R905.3.6

  1. Application
     - Tile applied based on:
       - Climate condition.
       - Roof slope.
       - Underlayment system.
       - Type of tile being installed.

       R905.3.7

     - Perimeter tiles shall be fastened with a minimum of one fastener per tile.

       R905.3.7

     - Fasteners shall be per manufacturers' instructions in areas where winds exceed 100 mph and on buildings where the roof is more than 40 feet (12 192 mm) above grade.

       R905.3.7

     - In snow areas, a minimum of two fasteners shall comply with Table R805.3.7.

       R905.3.7

CLAY AND CONCRETE TILE

METAL ROOF SHINGLES

2. Flashing

- At the juncture of vertical roof surfaces a No. 26 gage galvanized sheet shall be installed.

R905.3.8

- The valley flashing shall extend a minimum of 11 inches (279 mm) from center line with a minimum 1-inch (25 mm) splash diverter.

R905.3.8

- The end lap shall not be less than 4 inches (102 mm).

R905.3.8

- Special provisions shall apply for ice dams.

R905.3.8

C. Metal roof shingles

- Shingles shall be applied to a solid or closely fitted deck, except where specifically designed for spaced sheathing.

R905.4.1

- Shingles are not permitted on roof slopes less than 3:12.

R905.4.2

- Special provisions shall apply in areas where the average daily temperature in January is 25°F (-4°C) or less.

R905.4.3

- Fasteners shall comply with the manufacturers' instructions.

R905.4.5

- Flashing shall extend a minimum of 8 inches (203 mm) from centerline with a ¾-inch (19.1 mm) splash diameter.

R905.4.6

- The end and lap of flashing shall not be less than 4 inches (102 mm).

R905.4.6

- Special provisions shall apply in areas where the average daily temperature in January is 25°F (-4°C) or less.

R905.4.6

D. Mineral-surfaced roll roofing

- Roll roofing shall be fastened to solidly sheathed roofs.

R905.5.1

- Roofing shall be applied to roofs with a minimum roof slope of 1:12.

R905.5.2

- Special provisions shall apply in areas where the average daily temperature in January is 25°F (-4°C) or less.
  R905.5.3
- Roofing shall be installed per manufacturers' instructions.
  R905.5.5

E. Slate and slate-type shingles

- Shingles shall be fastened to solidly sheathed roofs.
  R905.6.1
- Shingles shall be applied to roofs with a minimum roof slope of 4:12.
  R905.6.2
- Special provisions shall apply in areas where the average daily temperature in January is 25°F (-4°C) or less.
  R905.6.3
- The minimum headlap for slate shingles shall comply with Table R905.6.5.
  R905.6.5
- Two fasteners are required per slate.
  R905.6.5
- Flashing shall be made with sheet metal.
  R905.6.6

F. Wood shingles

- Shingles shall be placed on spaced or solid sheathing.
  R905.7.1
- A minimum of 1-inch by 4-inch (25 mm by 102 mm) boards shall be used for spaced sheathing, and shall be spaced equal to weather exposure.
  R905.7.1
- Special provisions shall apply in areas where the average daily temperature in January is 25°F (-4°C) or less.
  R905.7.1.1
- Shingles shall be applied to roofs with a slope of 3:12 or greater.
  R905.7.2
- Wood shingles shall comply with Table R905.7.4 for material requirements and Table R905.7.5 for weather exposure and roof slope.
  R905.7.4

WOOD SHINGLES

WOOD SHAKES

- Side lap shall not be less than 1½ inches (38 mm) between joints in courses; no two joints in any three adjacent courses shall align.

R905.7.5

- Shingles shall be laid with spacing of ¼ inch to ³/₈ inch (6.4 mm to 9.5 mm) between shingles.

R905.7.5

- Two fasteners are required per shingle, ¾ inch (19.1 mm) from edge, and no more than 1 inch (25 mm) above exposure line.

R905.7.5

- Fasteners shall be corrosion resistant, with a minimum penetration of ½ inch (12.7 mm) or through the sheathing.

R905.7.5

- A No. 26 gage corrosion-resistant flashing is required 10 inches (254 mm) from center line for slopes less than 12:12 and 7 inches (178 mm) from center line for roof slopes of 12:12.

R905.7.6

- Each bundle of shingles shall be identified by a label.

R905.7.7

G. Wood shakes

- Shakes shall only be used on solid or spaced sheathing.

R905.8.1

- 1-inch by 4-inch (25.4 mm by 102 mm) sheathing boards shall be used for spaced sheathing; if spaced 10 inches (254 mm) on center additional boards are required.

R905.8.1

- Special provisions shall apply in areas where the average daily temperature in January is 25°F (-4°C) or less.

R905.8.1.1

- Shakes shall only be applied on roofs with a minimum slope of 3:12 or greater.

R905.8.2

- Wood shakes shall comply with Table R905.8.5 for material requirements, and Table R905.8.6 for weather exposure and roof slope.

R905.8.5

117

- When shakes are laid with side lap, there shall be no less than 1 ½ inches (38 mm) between joints in courses.
  R905.8.6

- Spacing between shakes shall be $1/8$ inch to $5/8$ inch (3.2 mm to 15.9 mm) for shakes and taper sawn shakes of naturally durable wood.
  R905.8.6

- Spacing between shakes shall be ¼ inch to $3/8$ inch (6.4 mm to 9.5 mm) for preservatively treated shakes.
  R905.8.6

- Fasteners shall be corrosion resistant with a minimum penetration of ½ inch (12.7 mm) or through the sheathing.
  R905.8.6

- There shall be a minimum of two fasteners per shake, 1 inch (25 mm) from edge and no more than 2 inches (51 mm) above the exposure line.
  R905.8.6

- The starter course at ends shall be doubled.
  R905.8.7

- Flashing shall be a No. 26 gage, 11 inches (279 mm) from center line.
  R905.8.8

- Each bundle of shakes shall be identified by a label.
  R905.8.9

H. Built-up roofs

- Roofs shall have a minimum design slope of ¼:2 for drainage, except a slope of $1/8$:12 for coal tar.
  R905.9.1

- Materials shall comply with Table R905.9.2.
  R905.9.2

- Roofs shall be installed per manufacturers' installation instructions.
  R905.9.3

I. Metal roof panels

- Panels shall be applied to solid or spaced sheathing, except where the roof covering is designed to be applied to spaced supports.
  R905.10.1

BUILT-UP ROOFS

MISCELLANEOUS ROOF COVERINGS

- The minimum roof slope shall be 3:12 for lapped, nonsoldered seam without lap sealant, and ½:12 for lapped, nonsoldered seam with lap sealant.

R905.10.2

- The minimum roof slope shall be ¼:12 for standing seam roof systems.

R905.10.2

- Materials shall comply with Table R905.10.3.

R905.10.3

- Metal roofing shall be fastened directly to steel framing with approved fasteners:
  1. Galvanized fasteners for galvanized roofs.
  2. Hard copper or copper alloy for copper roofs.
  3. Stainless steel.

R905.10

J. Modified bitumen roofing

- Roofing shall have a minimum design slope of ¼:12.

R905.11.1

- Material shall comply with Table R905.11.2.

R905.11.2

- Roofing shall be installed per Chapter 9 and the manufacturers' instructions.

R905.11.3

K. Thermoset single-ply roofing

- Roofing shall have a minimum design slope of ¼:12.

R905.12.1

- Roofing shall be installed per Chapter 9 and the manufacturers' instructions.

R905.12.3

L. Thermoplastic single-ply roofing

- Roofing shall have a minimum design slope of ¼:12.

R905.13.1

- Roofing shall be installed per Chapter 9 and the manufacturers' instructions.

R905.13.2

M. Sprayed polyurethane foam roofing

- Roofing shall have a minimum design slope of ¼:12.
R905.14.1

- Roofing shall be installed per Chapter 9 and the manufacturers' instructions.
R905.14.3

- Liquid-applied protective coating complying with Section R905.5 shall be applied no less than 2 hours and no more than 72 hours following the application of foam.
R905.14.3

- Foam plastic materials and installation shall comply with Section R318.
R905.14.4

N. Liquid-applied coatings

- Roofing shall have a minimum design slope of ¼:12.
R905.15.1

- Roofing shall be installed per Chapter 9 and the manufacturers' instructions.
R905.15.3

V. Roof Insulation

- Above deck thermal insulation shall be applied when covered by approved roof covering.
R906.1

VI. Reroofing

- Roof repairs to existing roofs and roof coverings shall comply with Chapter 9. See exception.
R907.1

- Existing roof coverings shall be removed if any of the following occur:
    1. Existing roof or roof covering is water-soaked or has deteriorated.
    2. Existing roof is wood shake, slate, clay, cement or asbestos-cement tile.
    3. Existing roof has two or more applications of any type of roof covering.
R907.3

REROOFING

- New roof coverings over wood shingle or wood shake roofs that create a combustible concealed space are required to have existing surface covered with gypsum board, mineral fiber, glass fiber or other approved materials.

R907.4

- Approved roofing coverings and flashing are permitted to be reused.

R907.5

- Aggregate surfacing materials shall not be reinstalled.

R907.5

- Flashings shall be reconstructed per the manufacturers' instructions.

R907.6

CHIMNEYS AND FIREPLACES

I. Masonry Chimneys

- Masonry and concrete chimneys in SDC D_1 and D_2 shall be reinforced and anchored per Section R1003.
R1001.1

- Reinforcement and seismic anchorage are not required in SDC A, B and C.
R1001.1

- Foundations of solid masonry or concrete shall be a minimum of 12 inches (305 mm) thick and at least 6 inches (152 mm) beyond each side.
R1001.1.1

- Foundations shall be placed a minimum of 12 inches (305 mm) below grade in areas not subject to freezing.
R1001.1.1

- Masonry chimney corbelling is limited.
R1001.2

- Chimney wall or flue lining shall not change in size or shape within 6 inches (152 mm) above or below floor, ceiling or roof components.
R1001.3

- Offsets are limited.
R1001.4

- Unless designed, chimneys shall not support loads other than their own weight; chimneys shall be constructed as part of masonry or reinforced walls.
R1001.5

- Chimneys shall extend a minimum of 2 feet (610 mm) above any portion of a building within 10 feet (3048 mm), but no less than 3 feet (914 mm) above the roof.
R1001.6

A. Spark arrestors, where installed

- The net free area of the arrestor shall be no less than four times the net free area of the chimney flue outlet.
R1001.6.1

- Arrestor shall have a corrosion and heat resistance equal to 19-gage galvanized steel or 24-gage stainless steel.
R1001.6.1

MASONRY CHIMNEYS

MASONRY CHIMNEYS

- Openings shall not allow the passage of spheres greater than ½ inch (12.7 mm) and shall not block spheres less than $^3/_8$ inch (9.5 mm).

R1001.6.1

- Arrestors shall be accessible and removable for cleaning.

R1001.6.1

- The minimum wall thickness of a chimney shall be 4 inches (102 mm).

R1001.7

- Masonry chimneys shall be lined; specific requirements apply to:
  Residential-type appliances.

R1001.8.1

  Special appliances.

R1001.8.2

  Gas appliances.

R1001.8.3

  Pellet fuel-burning appliances.

R1001.8.4

  Oil-fired appliances, Type L vent.

R1001.8.5

- A notice of usage is required when the flue is lined with noncomplying material.

R1001.8.6

B. Flue lining installation

- Lining shall extend from a point no less than 8 inches (203 mm) below the lowest inlet or smoke chamber to a point above the enclosing walls.

R1001.9

- Flue lining shall be vertical, with a maximum slope no greater than 30 degrees from vertical.

R1001.9

- Flue liner shall be supported on all sides.

R1001.9

- Listed materials used as flue liners shall be installed per the manufacturers' instructions.

R1001.9

- The space surrounding the chimney lining system shall not be used to vent any other appliance. See exception.

R1001.9

- Masonry wythes are required between two or more flues located in the same chimney and shall be at least 4 inches (102 mm) thick. See exception.

   R1001.10

C. Flue area

- Flue areas shall not be smaller in area than the area of the connector from the appliance.

   R1001.11

- Round flue sizes shall comply with Table R1001.11(1).

   R1001.11

- Square and rectangular flue sizes shall comply with Table R1001.11(2).

   R1001.11

- Masonry fireplaces' flue area shall comply with Section R1001.12.1 or R1011.12.2.

   R1001.11

  1. Option 1
     - Round flue shall have a minimum net cross-sectional area of one-twelfth the fireplace opening.

        R1001.12.1

     - Square flues shall have a minimum net cross-sectional area of one-tenth or one-eighth based on the aspect ratio.

        R1001.12.1

  2. Option 2
     - Size is determined by Figure R1001.12.2; cross-sectional area of clay flue linings shall comply with Tables R1001.11(1) and R1001.11(2) or per the manufacturers' instructions.

        R1001.12.2

     - Height of chimney shall be measured from the firebox floor to the top of the flue.

        R1001.12.2

D. Inlets

- Inlets shall enter from the side.

   R1001.13

- Inlets shall have a thimble of fireclay, rigid refactory material or metal.

   R1001.13

MASONRY CHIMNEYS

MASONRY CHIMNEYS

E. Cleanouts—masonry chimneys

- Cleanout openings shall be located within 6 inches (152 mm) of the base of each flue.

R1001.14

- The upper edge of cleanout openings shall be located at least 6 inches (152 mm) below the lowest chimney inlet opening.

R1001.14

- The minimum height of the openings shall be 6 inches (152 mm).

R1001.14

- A noncombustible cover is required.

R1001.14

- A cover is not required where cleaning is possible through the fireplace opening.

R1001.14

F. Chimney clearances

- A 2-inch (51 mm) minimum air space clearance to combustibles is required when located inside the buildings or within the exterior wall.

R1001.15

- A 1-inch (25 mm) minimum air space clearance is required when located outside the exterior walls.

R1001.15

- Air space shall not be filled except to provide fireblocking. See exceptions.

R1001.15

G. Chimney fireblocking

- All spaces between floors and ceilings shall be blocked with noncombustible materials.

R1001.16

- Spaces between chimneys and wood joists, beams or headers shall have a minimum depth of 1 inch (25 mm), and shall be placed on strips of metal or metal lath.

R1001.16

- H. Chimney crickets
- Crickets are required when the dimension parallel to ridgeline exceeds 30 inches (762 mm) and does not intersect with the ridgeline.

    R1001.17

- Flashing and counterflashing are required.

    R1001.17

- Crickets shall comply with Figure R1001.17 and Table R1001.17.

    R1001.17

II. Factory-built Chimneys

- Chimneys are required to be listed and labeled.

    R1002.1

- Decorative shrouds shall not be used unless listed and labeled.

    R1001.2

- Solid-fuel-burning appliances shall comply with Type HT requirements of UL 103. See exceptions.

    R1002.3

- Factory-built chimneys for medium-heat appliances shall comply with UL 959.

    R1002.6

III. Masonry Fireplaces

- Foundations shall be a minimum of 12 inches (305 mm) thick and extend at least 6 inches (152 mm) beyond all sides.

    R1003.2

- Footings shall be at least 12 inches (305 mm) below the finished grade or below the frost line.

    R1003.2

- Footings shall be on natural, undisturbed earth or engineered fill.

    R1003.2

- A. Ash dump cleanout
- Openings shall be equipped with ferrous metal or masonry doors.

    R1003.2.1

- Doors are to close tight when they are not in use.

    R1003.2.1

FACTORY-BUILT CHIMNEYS

MASONRY FIREPLACES

- Cleanouts shall be accessible and located so removal of ash does not create a hazard to combustible materials.

R1003.2.1

- Masonry or concrete chimneys in SDC D₁ and D₂ shall be reinforced.

R1003.2.1

- Reinforcement shall comply with Table R1003.1 and Section R609.

R1003.3

- Four No. 4 continuous vertical rebar for chimneys up to 40 inches (1016 mm) wide are required; for chimneys over 40 inches (1016 mm) two additional No. 4 rebars are required.

R1003.3.1

- For horizontal reinforcement, ¼-inch (6.4 mm) ties shall be used in bed joints a minimum of every 18 inches (457 mm) of vertical height. Two ties shall be placed at each bend in vertical bars.

R1003.3.2

B. Seismic anchorage (SDC D₁ and D₂)

- Chimneys shall be anchored at each floor, ceiling or roof line more than 6 feet (1829 mm) above grade.

R1003.4

- Two ³/₁₆-inch by 1-inch (4.8 mm by 25 mm) straps shall be embedded a minimum of 12 inches (305 mm) into the chimney.

R1003.4.1

- Straps shall be hooked around the outer bars and extend 6 inches (152 mm) beyond the bend.

R1003.4.1

- Straps shall be fastened to a minimum of four floor joists, ceiling joists or rafters with two ½-inch (12.7 mm) bolts.

R1003.4

C. Firebox walls

- Walls shall be a minimum of 8 inches (203 mm) thick if the firebrick lining is 2 inches (51 mm) thick.

R1003.5

- The maximum width of joints shall be ¼ inch (6.4 mm).

R1003.5

127

- If the firebrick does not have lining, the minimum thickness of the back and side walls shall be 10 inches (254 mm).

    R1003.5

  1. Steel fireplace units
     - The firebox liner, where provided, shall not be less than ¼ inch (6.4 mm) steel.

        R1003.5

     - Firebox shall be encased in 8 inches (203 mm) of solid masonry for back and side walls, of which no less than 4 inches (102 mm) shall be solid masonry.

        R1003.5

     - Warm-air ducts shall be metal or masonry.

        R1003.5.1

D. Firebox dimensions

- The firebox of a concrete or masonry firebox shall have a 20 inch (508 mm) depth.

    R1003.6

- The throat shall not be less than 8 inches (203 mm) above the fireplace opening and not less than 4 inches (102 mm) in depth.

    R1003.6

- The firebox shall be no less than the cross-sectional area of the flue. See exception.

    R1003.6

E. Lintel and throat

- A noncombustible lintel is required.

    R1003.7

- A 4-inch (102 mm) minimum bearing shall be provided on each end of the fireplace.

    R1003.7

- The fireplace throat or damper shall be located a minimum of 8 inches (203 mm) above the lintel.

    R1003.7

F. Smoke chamber

- Corbelling shall not leave cores exposed inside the chamber.

    R1003.8

- The chamber shall be 6 inches (152 mm) thick when using firebrick or vitrified clay lining.

    R1003.8

MASONRY FIREPLACES

MASONRY FIREPLACES

- If the chamber is without lining, the solid masonry shall be a minimum of 8 inches (203 mm).

R1003.8

- Parging is required when the inside surface is corbelled.

R1003.8

- The height of the smoke chamber shall not be greater than the fireplace opening.

R1003.8.1

- The inside surface shall not incline more than 45 degrees when the chamber is rolled or sloped.

R1003.8.1

- Walls shall not be corbelled more than 30 degrees.

R1003.8.1

G. Hearth and hearth extension

- Hearths shall be constructed of concrete or masonry, with no combustible materials remaining after construction.

R1003.9

- 4 inches (102 mm) shall be the minimum thickness for hearths.

R1003.9.1

- 2 inches (51 mm) shall be the minimum thickness for hearth extensions. See exceptions.

R1003.9.2

- Hearths shall extend 16 inches (406 mm) in front and 8 inches (203 mm) beyond each side.

R1003.10

- A fireplace opening 6 square feet (.56 m^2) or greater shall extend a minimum of 20 inches (508 mm) in front and 12 inches (305 mm) beyond each side.

R1003.10

H. Fireplace clearance

- All combustibles shall be no less than 2 inches (51 mm) away from the front and sides of fireplaces.

R1003.11

- All combustibles shall be no less than 4 inches (102 mm) from the back of masonry fireplaces.

R1003.11

- Air space shall not be filled except to provide fireblocking. See exceptions.

   R1003.11

I. Mantel and trim

- Combustibles shall not be placed within 6 inches (152 mm) of the fireplace opening.

   R1003.12

- Combustibles within 12 inches (304 mm) of the fireplace opening shall not project more than $1/8$ inch (3.2 mm) for each 1 inch (25 mm) distance from opening.

   R1003.13

IV. Factory-built Fireplaces

- Fireplaces shall be listed and labeled.

   R1004.1

- The hearth extension shall be installed per listing and readily distinguishable from the surrounding floor area.

   R1004.2

- Decorative shrouds shall not be used unless listed and labeled.

   R1004.3

- An unvented gas log shall not be used unless listed and labeled.

   R1004.4

V. Exterior Air Supply

- An exterior air supply is required unless the mechanical system provides neutral or positive indoor air pressure.

   R1005.1

- Exterior combustion air ducts for factory-built fireplaces shall be listed components.

   R1005.1.1

- Listed combustion air ducts are required for masonry fireplaces.

   R1005.1.2

- Exterior air intake shall be capable of providing all combustion air.

   R1005.2

FACTORY-BUILT FIREPLACES

EXTERIOR AIR SUPPLY

- Exterior air intake shall not be located within a garage or basement, nor at an elevation higher than the firebox.
R1005.2

- Exterior air intake shall be covered with corrosion-resistant screen of ¼ inch (6.4 mm) mesh.
R1005.2

- A minimum 1-inch (25 mm) clearance from combustibles is required for all unlisted combustion air ducts within 5 feet (1524 mm) of the duct outlet.
R1005.3

- The combustion air passageway shall be a minimum of 6 square inches (.004 m^2) and a maximum of 55 square inches (.035 m^2), unless listed.
R1005.4

- An exterior air outlet is required to be located in the back or sides of the firebox chamber or within 24 inches (610 mm) of the firebox opening.
R1005.5

- The exterior air outlet shall be closeable and designed to prevent burning materials from dropping into concealed combustible spaces.
R1005.5

VI. Masonry Heaters

- Heaters shall be installed per listing or ASTM E 1602.
R1006.1

- A minimum clearance of 4 inches (100 mm) is required to the adjacent framing.
R1006.2

- Reinforcement is not required in SDC A, B and C.
R1006.2

- Reinforcement is required to anchor the masonry heater to the foundation in SDC D$_1$ and D$_2$.
R1006.2

- Reinforcement is required when the masonry chimney and facing of masonry heater share a common wall.
R1006.2